What Others Are S...
Rent-to-B...

"We've known Wendy Patton for years and she's one of the best at creative financing. 'Rent-to-Buy' is a timely book designed to help aspiring buyers and the agents who support them find a solution in a tough market."
Gary Keller, best-selling author of _"The Millionaire Real Estate Agent"_ and _"SHIFT: How Top Real Estate Agents Tackle Tough Times"_

"Wendy Patton has come out with another masterpiece. Her reputation as an investor and educator is stellar and any book she writes you must read. Whether you are a first time homebuyer looking for a great deal on your personal residence or a full time investor looking for a great way to acquire more properties this is a must read. Right now the real estate market is a perfect storm for what Wendy teaches you in this book."
**Than Merrill – Star of A&E's "Flip this House"
and Founder of FortuneBuilders.com**

"Bulls-eye! The target has been hit dead center again. As a Realtor®, this provides an avenue of option to 'own the American dream'."
**Kathleen Sanchez
Associate Broker/Owner
Coldwell Banker Shooltz**

"Thank you, Wendy! Perfect timing for this must-read book! It shows real estate professionals how to creatively put future buyers into homes, thus reducing the number of homes needing buyers, and ultimately adding sales for the real estate agent! 'Rent-to-Buy' is the perfect complement to Wendy's 'Rent-to-Sell'."
**Steve Giroux, Realtor®
Keller Williams**

"Wendy's Patton's 'Rent-to-Buy' is a must read book for all Realtors® and home buyers. It could not come at a better time! With foreclosures at an all time high and mortgage changes occurring almost daily, Buyer's need every advantage available to them to purchase homes, and 'Rent-to-Buy' will be the answer to their prayers.

Buyers are an integral part of a Realtor's business and any bit of education; idea, or creative method that can get a buyer into a home is extremely beneficial. 'Rent-to-Buy' gives us a jump-start ahead of the competition to help buyers acquire their dream home."
Bill Janiga
Real Estate Consultant / Investor
RE/MAX Home Sale Services

"As a new college graduate entering the home market, I couldn't get a mortgage to buy a house. Instead, I rented to own, eventually buying the property when my job and credit history allowed. With today's "credit crunch", this strategy has become even more timely, and Wendy Patton shows you the best ways to start on the path to home ownership. All the pros, all the cons, and what you should know BEFORE you sign the contract are right here. This book is required reading for anyone even thinking about renting to buy."
Vena Jones-Cox
Owner of RealLifeRealEstate.com

"Wendy's 'Rent-to-Buy' is a great way learn how to acquire a house in creative ways"
William Bronchick,
Attorney & Best-Selling Author

"Wendy's 'Rent-to-Buy' is the perfect complement to her 'Rent-to-Sell'. Since implementing her strategies, I have been empowered to help more people buy and sell real estate. It is nice to be able to get excited about real estate again!"
Theresa Blahut,
GRI Broker-Associate
Charles Rutenberg Realty, Orlando, FL

"We are all aware of the challenges of today's market; many of us also see the opportunity in today's market. Wendy clearly lays out a very detailed action plan to help us grab this unique opportunity. The timing of this book is incredible and it is a MUST READ by anyone looking to buy a home in today's market!"
Mark Prinz
General Manager – Select Realty (Mississippi & Michigan)
www.msselectrealty.com

"Wendy's timing couldn't be better! This book is an informative 'how-to' manual for buyers seeking creative financing. I not only give this to my buyer clients, but to my sellers as well. What a great way to open their eyes to alternative marketing strategies!"
Debbie Kessler
Associate Broker
Century 21 Real Estate 217

Rent-to-Buy

Your Hands-On Guide to BUY Your Home

When Mortgage Lending is Tight

By: Wendy Patton

Featuring Dozens of Ideas to Rebuild Credit

While Buying Your Dream Home

AuthorHouse™
1663 Liberty Drive
Bloomington, IN 47403
www.authorhouse.com
Phone: 1-800-839-8640

First published by AuthorHouse 10/13/2009

ISBN: 978-1-4490-0096-7 (sc)

Library of Congress Control Number: 2009910769

Printed in the United States of America
Bloomington, Indiana

This book is printed on acid-free paper.

authorHOUSE®

Table of Contents

Dedication

This book is dedicated to all of the buyers in North America that want to buy their first home or next home, but just can't do it. Unfortunately, the mortgage industry has changed along with the economy. It is affecting and squeezing every buyer and seller in our country. I congratulate you for picking up this book and researching how you can be a home owner in the near future. Home ownership is within your reach if you really want it.

This book is also dedicated to the real estate professionals that must change the way they do business in order to survive this real estate downturn. Congratulations to you for picking up this book and making a change in your business approach.

I want to give special thanks to so many people that helped me with this book. Robert Golden, I couldn't do it without you! To my friends and colleagues Merrilee Anderson, Brenda Brendel and Veronica Johnstone who helped me with reading and proofing my writing over and over again, thanks. To my husband, Michael, who has to put up without me during the time I am writing. I appreciate you all so much.

Introduction

Let me paint a picture for you. You've seen tons of homes for sale on the market. You know it's a buyer's market. You either owned a home previously or you are a first time buyer. If you owned a home previously you might have lost it to foreclosure, either due to a job loss, divorce or your mortgage rate adjusting upwards.

Now is the time to buy! After all, you keep hearing in the news about how BAD things are for sellers, and prices are the lowest they've been in years. This is true and it is to your advantage. For most of us, home ownership is our single, biggest source of wealth. It not only puts a roof over our heads that we can call our own, but it also builds security for our futures by paying down the mortgage and building up equity. For most people, their home is their single greatest asset.

Probably the first thing you did was to start looking on the Internet or checking the local newspaper for homes for sale. After that, you called a Realtor® and he told you that he would love to help you, but you needed to get approved for a mortgage first. Ugh...you know you don't have the best of credit and you are not sure if you should even call a mortgage lender.

You decide to make the call to a mortgage lender. You know what the outcome will most likely be in advance, because of your financial situation, but you do it anyway. After gathering tons of information from you all the way down to how many times a week you floss, he finally tells you that based on your current credit, income, down payment, inadequate amount of time spent brushing after meals, etc. you aren't currently qualified to get a mortgage. Well, duh! You could have told him that in the first place. Do not despair.

Whether you owned a home before that was foreclosed on, you were a renter or you are a first-time buyer, chances are if you are reading this you have already experienced the above scenario, or at least something close to it.

The problem is that at the same time, rents are starting to go up in many areas of the country as the demand for rentals has increased. How much money do you want to continue forking over each month in rent only to pay the landlord's mortgage? You want to BUY a home. That's why you've been looking, and why you are reading this book.

Most people would give up here, despite the increasing rents. After all, if you can't get a mortgage, you can't buy a home, right? But we both know you aren't most people. You have taken the step to educate yourself by buying this book. The banks want you to forget that there are ways to buy homes other than just getting a mortgage – you DO have options. Heck, even if you CAN qualify for a mortgage right now, you might be looking for another option just to give yourself some leeway in this difficult housing market. This book is all about giving you another option, a way to get into your new home now, even if you can't qualify for the loan yet.

What this is, of course, is a guide for buying your next home without having to have a mortgage right away, without having to have perfect credit and without having to have a large down payment. This is a guide to a creative home buying technique known as "rent-to-own" or "lease-option."

Last year, the National Association of Realtors® (NAR) reported that the current month's supply of homes across the nation is 9.9 months. That means at the current pace of sales, it will take 9.9 months to sell all of the homes on the market. A stable real estate market typically has about 6 months supply, which means we've got an extra 4 months of surplus homes to get sold. That's a lot of competition for the small pool of buyers out there, which you are a part of.

Naturally, more homes are coming on the market and it looks like it's only going to get worse for a while as the foreclosure volume from the subprime mess is still increasing. In fact, RealtyTrac™ reported that in the 1st quarter of last year, foreclosure filings were up 116% over the 1st quarter of the previous year.

Homeowners and banks aren't the only ones trying to sell their homes. The new home builders overbuilt in many areas, resulting in lots of brand new homes that they are getting desperate to sell. They need buyers and they need them now. Throw the builders into the mix and the picture gets better and better for the buyer doesn't it?

Where are all of the buyers? If it were a reality TV show, they would call it "Lost! The Search for America's Home Buyers." Buying your home on a rent-to-own basis is nothing new. People have been doing it for decades. We aren't inventing the wheel here; it's just that it's become a little less commonplace in the last decade or so. The reason for this is very simple – for the last decade the banks made it their personal goal to give a mortgage to every man, woman and child on the face of the earth that could pass one simple test – could they fog a mirror when they breathed on it? As long as the applicant was alive, the banks didn't see any reason to bother with little things like income, down payment, an appraisal based on reality, etc.

Naturally, the "everyone is qualified for a mortgage" couldn't last forever. From the massive volume of "For Sale" signs plastered on front lawns we can see that it hasn't. Now, the banks are only willing to give mortgages to applicants that can provide a 90% upfront down payment and are willing to give up their first born to indentured servitude until the loan is paid off.

I'm exaggerating, of course, but if you've been trying to qualify for a mortgage during this credit crunch, that's exactly what it feels like. The point I'm making is that it is much, MUCH harder to get a loan than it used to be and that's where all of the buyers have gone. They've either tried to get a loan and couldn't or got scared off by all of the media sensationalism about how bad the market is and how hard it is to get a loan.

You might be thinking that because you can't qualify for a mortgage right now you will only be able to get a rent-to-own home from the most desperate sellers with the ugliest, most over-priced house. While it's true that those are going to be some of the homes available on a rent-to-own basis, you'll be happy to know that they are far from being the only ones. It's also possible to buy homes in excellent condition, even fully renovated homes or new construction, on a rent-to-own basis - and still pay fair market price! Remember, it's a buyer's market in most of the country and that's going to help offset the fact that you can't qualify for a mortgage right now.

As I said, renting to own has become a little less commonplace, but it's time to dust it off and put it back into mainstream practice. In the upcoming chapters I will teach you what rent-to-own is, how it works and lots of other tips and tricks for buying your next home without qualifying for a mortgage or having a huge down payment.

Before we jump into all of the details though, you are probably wondering how hard this is going to be. You are probably wondering if this is something you can do on your own or if buying this book is going to be a big waste of money. Since you've been patient enough to read through this whole introduction, I'm going to reward you with that answer. If you happen to have skipped ahead right to the end of the introduction, you sneaky devil you, you're in luck - you'll get the answer too…

Seriously though, I have been doing rent-to-own deals for more than 20 years. That's right, I was doing them before the bankers convinced all of the sellers that only buyers with conventional loans should get homes. Yes, I still did them while the banks were trying to fulfill their goal of eliminating all renters on the planet by digging themselves into the subprime pit of doom. Fortunately for me, I outlived a lot of these banks. Not only have I been doing rent-to-own transactions through all of this, but I've also been teaching others to do them as well. I have taught more than 20,000 people from all walks of life, and I can assure you that I wouldn't still be teaching if it couldn't be learned.

So if you've already bought this book, go ahead and get comfortable in your favorite chair, put your feet up and we'll get started. If you haven't bought the book yet, but you want to buy your next home, trust me, this book will come in VERY handy. In fact, given the current credit crunch, it just may be the only way you'll get to buy your home right now. Go ahead and proceed to the cashier and fork over your credit card. You will not regret it!

Wendy

PART 1:

WHAT IS
RENT-TO-OWN
AND HOW DOES IT WORK?

Chapter 1:

What is Rent-to-Own

Before we can look at why we would want to buy a home and how to buy a home on a "rent-to-own" basis, we first need to understand what renting-to-own is. A rent-to-own can also be referred to as a "Lease with an Option to Buy," a "Lease Option" or a "Lease to Own." In this book we will call it a "Rent-to-Own", but these words can be used interchangeably for the most part.

In a nutshell, a rent-to-own sale means the seller is allowing you, the future buyer, to live in the home for a while as a renter before you actually purchase the home from them.

In a rent-to-own transaction, before you move into the seller's home as a renter, you and the seller would agree on the sale price and other terms. You would pay the seller a non-refundable *option fee*. Both you and the seller would sign some paperwork covering the lease, the purchase and the *option* (which gives you the right to purchase the home at a later date) and in approximately one to three years, depending on your agreement, you have the *option* of purchasing the home.

I say you have the *option* of purchasing the home because it is important to understand that in a rent-to-own transaction you, as the buyer, *are not obligated to purchase the home* at the end of the rental period. The seller, however, is required to sell it to you should you choose to buy it. That sounds pretty good, doesn't it?

Wendy's Wisdom

A rent-to-own transaction does NOT require you to buy the home. However, if you don't buy, the seller does get to keep your option fee.

In later chapters we will go into great detail about the whole process. Right now I just want you to have a foundation of understanding about renting-to-own. Let's recap.

A rent-to-own transaction between you (the tenant-buyer) and a seller is comprised of paperwork and contracts, which include:

- A Sales Contract containing the price

- An Option Agreement which contains the time period and option fee amount

- A rental period agreement

What you need to remember is that even though you will be signing a Sales Contract, it remains your choice to purchase the home, not an obligation to buy it. You are, however, also guaranteed the right to buy it, if you wish to, and you are financially ready to qualify for the mortgage. An exclusive right to purchase is what your option fee provides for you.

Why Would I Need to do This Rent-to-Own thing?

This, of course, brings up two questions:

    1. "Why in the world would the seller let me do this?"

    2. "Why would I need to do this?"

If we take a look at the condition of our current housing market, we'll find some answers.

The Realities of our Current Housing Market – Can You Say "Slump"?

Let's face it; throughout much of the country, the real estate market is tough for sellers. Many areas went through a period of real estate insanity that will be looked back on as the "Boom" years. The Boom years gave us double-digit appreciation rates and home values soared in much of the country. Some areas were so crazy that the appreciation rates were as much as 40% or more in one year. In Miami, Florida, the median selling price of a home in January of 2003 was about $190,000. By January of 2007, the median selling price was $375,000! That's about 100% appreciation in 4 years, or 25% per year.

Do you think that appreciation rates of 25% per year are realistic? I'm sure you have heard the saying, "What goes up, must come down."

Note

Not everywhere in the country was seeing such glamorous home price increases. In Southeastern Michigan, where I live, from January 2003 to January of 2007, home values DROPPED by 2%.

With home prices surging so rapidly, people were buying them like the Nintendo Wii for Christmas. It was a mad rush to buy. Buyers were frantic to be a part of it because they wanted to capitalize on that crazy appreciation themselves. Those fabulous

Boom years were great for Realtors® and sellers; but tough on buyers. A real estate agent could get a listing and start putting the sign out front. Before he finished putting that sign in the ground, a buyer would drive up and start writing a deposit check – without even looking inside. Before that buyer could finish writing the check, another buyer would drive up and start writing a bigger deposit check for more than the asking price. A "For Sale" sign attracted buyers, almost like my cats when they hear the can opener!

If a buyer happened to buy early enough, he could take advantage of that great appreciation. If he bought at the top of his market, he had nowhere to go but down.

The simple fact of the matter is that the staggering appreciation rates that most areas experienced just weren't sustainable. The real estate market in most areas has not settled back down to mere mortal levels; they've dropped below that. Home selling prices in Miami, Florida, between January of 2007 and May of 2008, dropped from a median price of $375,000 to $340,000. By September of 2008, the median selling price dropped to $275,000. That's more than a $100,000 drop in just over 1½ years! It's still going down as of the writing of this book.

Miami is more of an extreme case than most of the country, both going up and coming down, but it does serve as a good example of how things have changed. Markets have changed to heavily favor buyers. That's why it's such a good time to buy now. That's why sellers need to find creative ways to sell their homes, like rent-to-own.

The problem for sellers is that qualified buyers have become scarce, just like my cats when they found out I only opened a can of green beans, and sellers are popping up everywhere. It seems like "For Sale" signs on the front lawns are now part of the landscaping that everyone plants when they put in their spring flowers.

It seems like these signs are everywhere.

It seems like these signs are all too scarce right now.

"For Sale" signs seem to be lingering well after the spring flowers have wilted. Whether your market is like Miami and is plummeting or your local market is much more moderate, odds are it's still much tougher for home sellers to sell now than it was just a couple of years ago. Most of the country is in a housing "slump".

So you're probably thinking, "Great! This makes it an excellent time for me to buy. Prices are low, sellers are competing for buyers, what more could I ask for?" All of that is true; however, there is just one teensy-tiny problem. While this housing slump is making it tough for home sellers, there is a balancing factor that's making it tough for home buyers. I call it the "Credit Crunch".

How the "Credit Crunch" Affects You – the Buyer

With the severe tightening of the mortgage lending industry, buyers are having a harder time getting mortgages. The subprime mess we've all heard about means that many buyers who could qualify for mortgages before are no longer able to. This may be your situation.

During the "Boom Years," lenders were putting buyers into Adjustable Rate Mortgages, or A.R.M.'s, meaning their interest rate would be adjusting after the introductory period, thereby increasing (possibly decreasing, but not likely) their payment. They did this because the buyer couldn't qualify for a standard mortgage or even if he could qualify, he couldn't afford the payment because the interest rate on the 30-year fixed mortgage was so much higher. These adjustable rate mortgages are one type of a subprime loan.

The lenders reasoned that it was okay to give buyers these loans because home prices were appreciating so rapidly. The thought was that by the time the new homeowner's mortgage was getting close to adjusting upwards, the home would have appreciated enough that the owner could refinance into a conventional fixed rate mortgage.

Unfortunately, the rapid appreciation didn't continue forever and the homeowners discovered that not only could they not refinance their loan into a fixed rate, but they also could not afford the payments when their current loan adjusted upwards. The resulting impact is the highest number of home foreclosures in our nation's history!

With so many loans going into foreclosure, a number of smaller lenders went bankrupt and some of the larger lenders have stopped writing mortgages altogether. The lenders that continue to provide loans are being much more conservative, instituting much stricter guidelines, resulting in a serious "Credit Crunch".

This "Credit Crunch" directly impacts you as a potential homebuyer. Unless you have A+ credit or a very large down payment, getting a mortgage may prove difficult. If you haven't already spoken with a mortgage broker, you should do so to find out if you can currently qualify for a mortgage. If you have already spoken with a mortgage broker and you know you can't qualify yet, you know about this "Credit Crunch".

Many would-be buyers despair after talking to a real estate agent and a mortgage broker who tell them that they can't help them because they can't qualify right now. This is why you, as a buyer, would need to do something like rent-to-own. It gives you the opportunity to get into your future home now, before you can qualify for a mortgage.

Wendy's Wisdom

Don't give up hope if you can't qualify for a mortgage right now. This is an excellent time to buy a rent-to-own home!

Yes, you do have several choices when it comes to buying your new home! Obviously, this is the part where I sing the praises of rent-to-own.

Rent-to-Own, your Lifesaver in a Drowning Market

While most other buyers are drowning in the "Credit Crunch", you have a choice. Renting-to-own can allow you to buy your next home, even at a time when financing is so hard to obtain; but that's not the only advantage it offers. Let's take a look at some of the reasons why rent-to-own can be beneficial for you:

1. **Flexibility.** This is key. If you live in an uncertain market, you have the ability to get into your home now and still have the flexibility whether or not you want to buy. For most of you, buying is what you truly want and should plan for. Not buying is your "get out of jail card" if things don't go well for you personally. Don't go into a rent-to-own without being serious about purchasing the home.

2. **Time.** The rental period gives you time to improve your credit score and pay off some other debts or save more towards a larger down payment. It's very important to take advantage of this time by taking the proper steps. We will discuss credit repair in more detail later in the book.

3. **Option Credits.** One important negotiating point is having all or part of your monthly rental payment count

as a credit against the final purchase price. This is called an O*ption Credit,* and it can be an excellent way to increase your down payment and equity in your new home. For instance, if the rental payment is $1,200 per month and $600 of that gets applied towards buying the home (your *option credit*), you will build up $7,200 of equity for one year ($600 X 12 = $7,200). This will be covered in much more detail later in this book.

4. **Sweat Equity.** If you are a handyman and want to buy a fixer-upper home on a rent-to-own basis, you can build *Sweat Equity* in the home by making improvements while you are a renter. Once you purchase the home, these improvements will increase the appraised value of the home in comparison to your contracted purchase price. Having an equity spread (the home is worth more than you are buying it for) can be very helpful when you are obtaining financing. You will also want to consider asking the seller for *option credits* if you do certain repairs. For instance, if a repair is worth $3,000 but you can do it for $800, consider asking for a $3,000 credit from the seller. This would give you $2,200 in real value for your work, or *sweat equity.*

Wendy's Wisdom

Buying a rent-to-own home offers a lot of benefits to you: Flexibility, the ability to live in the home before you buy it, being able to accumulate a down payment while you live in the home and much more!

My Market Isn't Drowning; Can I Still Buy a Rent-to-Own Home?

If you live in a stable market or even a seller's market, it is still possible to buy a rent-to-own home. Although, in a seller's market it can be a little more challenging because there would be fewer sellers willing to consider selling their home on a rent-to-own basis. I have done rent-to-own deals and taught people to do them in all kinds of markets. Don't let the fact that you live in a seller's market intimidate you from trying. If you do live in a seller's market, that means homes are appreciating in value; so by locking in a price now, your new home will be that much more valuable when you actually buy it. In Part 2 –"How to Search for a Home" we will go into detail on how to find your rent-to-own home. These techniques will apply to seller's markets as well as buyer's markets.

A Special Note about Working with Real Estate Agents

Most buyers work with real estate agents when it comes to finding a home. This is just smart practice because they can guide you through the home buying process and help you avoid many pitfalls along the way. Not to mention the fact that in MOST cases, the seller is the one paying the agent's commission, so you don't have to pay them anything for their help. According to the National Association of Realtors'® "2007 Profile of Home Buyers and Sellers," 85% of sellers received assistance from a real estate agent when selling their home. Think about that -- 85% of the homes for sale are listed with real estate agents! Unless you want to limit yourself to just 15% of the homes on the market, you'll need to work with an agent to find your new home.

A common mistake that many buyers make is in directly contacting the listing agent of a home they are interested in because they think that this is the only agent that can show them the home. The problem with this is that this agent represents the seller, not you. He will be all too happy to show you the home and handle the transaction because it means he is getting both sides of the commission, but that doesn't change the fact that he isn't representing you.

Instead of contacting an agent whose name is on the sign listing a home you are interested in, go to a local real estate brokerage and ask to speak with a BUYER'S AGENT, or you can email my office at Refer@WendyPatton.com and I can give you the name of a buyer's agent in your area who is familiar with rent-to-own (most are not). A buyer's agent's job will be to represent YOU, not the seller. Your agent will still be paid their commission by the seller. Your buyer's agent can show you any home that is listed on the market, even if it's listed with another agent.

Even though you want to buy your home on a rent-to-own basis, I recommend that you make use of a real estate agent when possible.

Not all real estate agents understand how rent-to-own works. A real estate agent's biggest concern with doing a rent-to-own transaction, despite whatever he might tell you, is how he gets paid his commission. We'll go over the details of how this works in Chapter 4 –"Using a Realtor®". Additionally, there is a section at the end of this book just for real estate agents. If you need to inform your buyer's agent about how rent-to-own works, start with the reassurance that he will still get paid and he'll jump on board. Then give him a copy of this book.

The reason I recommend making use of a Realtor® is that because they have access to such a large pool of homes for sale, they can be invaluable in helping you find the right rent-to-own home for you. The information available to them is not generally available to the public, nor is it easy to find. Using this book, they will also learn some tricks I know to find rent-to-own homes that are not listed as rent-to-own. This will give them the biggest inventory of homes for you to choose from.

When Will Rent-to-Own NOT Work?

While buying your home on a rent-to-own basis can be a great solution for you, it isn't the perfect solution for every situation.

There are times when buying your home on a rent-to-own basis won't work, though these largely depend on the seller and you. The following are reasons that rent-to-own would not work for you:

1. **You can't afford the home.** Even if you can afford the rental payment, you need to make sure you understand how much the end mortgage payment will be, including property taxes and homeowner's insurance. Sometimes the rental payment is much less than the mortgage payment because area rents don't match up to area home values. Total up the costs of living in that home as a home OWNER, not just a renter, and make sure that total payment will fit within your budget. You can work with a mortgage broker to help you determine how much home you can afford. Also see Chapter 3 –"House Hunting Basics".

   Sometimes your payment will be higher than rent once you buy, but don't let that scare you off as long as you can afford it. Homeownership is the best way to accumulate and save your wealth. If you are not a homeowner it is unlikely you can itemize your tax write offs. The tax benefits alone might make all the difference to you. In the long run, home ownership is usually the largest portion of a person's wealth. Don't let the opportunity to be a homeowner pass you by.

2. **You don't improve your credit while you are renting.** If your credit is damaged before going into the rent-to-own home, that's okay, but if you don't take the necessary steps to get your credit straightened out while you are living in the home, you won't be able to get a mortgage in the end. You *must* pay your bills on time. You also might need to do credit repair, which we'll discuss later, in Chapter 17.

3. **You overextend your credit during the rental period.** When you move into a new home it's quite common to want to decorate it with new furnishings. Beware of the pitfalls of adding financing to your debts for things like new dining room sets, sofas, appliances, large screen TVs or anything else. Just because the retailers are willing to extend credit to you doesn't mean the mortgage lender is going to do so when you want to buy your home. Even if you make payments on time, if you still have the debts when it comes time to buy, debts only hurt you. Even a monthly payment of as little as $25 per month can actually reduce the mortgage amount you can qualify for by thousands of dollars! Remember, the more debts you have stacked up in your name, the less home you can afford, no matter how good your credit is. Hold on to your good credit and keep your spending and debt accumulation to a minimum.

4. **You don't pay your rent on time or at all.** If you make late rental payments, the bank is not going to be inclined to give you a mortgage when you want to buy. Paying on time is <u>critical</u> to your success in getting a mortgage. Not to mention the fact that late rental payments might void your purchase agreement or option agreement depending on the terms. Not paying at all, obviously, will not only keep you from getting a mortgage, but it's also going to get you evicted. You will also lose your option fee.

There are also times when a seller will not be able to do a rent-to-own. Here are some examples:

1. **The seller can't provide a clear title.** If the seller can't sell his home right now because he can't provide a clear title, he can't sell it on a rent-to-own basis either. Selling

as a rent-to-own will give him extra time to remove obstructions to conveying the title, but he must clear them out. I do not recommend that you buy a home from a seller in this type of situation. It is a risk you don't need, and there are many other homes available without this risk from which you can choose.

2. **The seller owes more than the house is worth.** This doesn't make the sale impossible; but it does make it difficult. If the seller owes more than the house is worth, he would need to pay off the difference when you buy the home. The seller would need to bring money to the closing to make up the difference between what he owes on his mortgage and what you will pay for the house. If this is the case, you may want to insist the seller put that money into an escrow account so you know it is available when it comes time for you to buy. Another possibility would be that he overpays his monthly mortgage payments, so the difference would be covered by the end of the rental period. I do not recommend you buy from a seller in this situation, however. At the time you decide to purchase the home, the seller may or may not have the money to pay off the shortage. This would be a bad situation for you.

3. **The seller is in foreclosure.** If the seller has no way of making up past-due payments to the lender, he will not be able to sell his home as a rent-to-own. Note also that if the seller is able to bring his payments current, he MUST stay current during the option period. You certainly don't want to be making payments to a seller only to find out he isn't paying his mortgage! I will cover this situation and how you can protect yourself later in the book.

Wendy's Wisdom

If your seller is in a situation where he had to catch up on mortgage payments, you should be writing your rent checks <u>directly to the seller's lender</u>. You can either mail them to the seller and he can forward them on (so the seller has proof the payment is being made) or you can send the seller proof of payments. Another option is setting up an escrow account that you pay directly and then the escrow service pays the lender.

If you don't make any of the mistakes listed above and your seller is not in any of the situations I described, you should be able to buy your next home on a rent-to-own basis.

In the next chapter, we'll get into some of the nitty-gritty details about how rent-to-own works.

Chapter 2:

How Does Rent-to-Own Work?

There are many pieces to the puzzle that fit together to make a rent-to-own transaction.

Understanding Rent-to-Own

In Chapter 1, I was deliberately vague about how the rent-to-own process works so you wouldn't get bogged down in the details. It's time now to get into some of those details so you'll have a deeper understanding. We established that a rent-to-own transaction between a buyer and seller will consist of the contracts, an agreement on price and terms, an option fee, a rental period and the end sale. Let's look at each of those parts now. If you have already decided that this is too much for you, then give this book to your Realtor®. If you need a Realtor® who understands rent-to-own, please email my office at Refer@WendyPatton.com and I will refer you to an agent well-versed in rent-to-own. Let's jump into the details.

How Rent-to-Own Transactions are Structured

The Contracts

In any real estate transaction, contracts play a vital role. They define the rules of the transaction. A rent-to-own sale is no different, although there is a bit more paperwork required to cover the different aspects. The three contracts needed in a rent-to-own transaction are the *Rental Agreement,* the *Option Agreement* and the *Sales Contract.* I'm going to give you a brief overview of each contract here so that you have a better understanding. We will look at each one individually in even greater detail in Part 3: "Understanding the Paperwork".

Rental Agreement

The *Rental* or *Lease Agreement* is very much like the lease agreement when renting an apartment or home. It defines the term of the lease, dictating how long the renter can live in the property as well as the amount of monthly rent and security deposit. Additionally, all of the other general rules and conditions of the lease are covered, such as the number of people permitted to live in the property, whether pets are allowed, how many cars, how repairs are handled and so on.

Option Agreement

The O*ption Agreement* or O*ption to Purchase Agreement* gives the tenant-buyer the right to purchase the home from the seller at a later date. It specifies how long the option agreement is valid. It states how long the tenant-buyer has to execute the purchase and close on the home. The option agreement usually does NOT specify the purchase price or terms of the purchase. It does, however, specify the amount of the option fee and whether there is a monthly option credit (*option credits* are an agreed upon amount that will be credited toward the purchase price should the renter purchase the property as agreed).

The *Option Fee* is what makes the Option Agreement valid; however, it is not 100% necessary to make it valid. Remember, option fees are non-refundable, but security deposits are refundable. Signing the *Rental Agreement*, which is *a promise to pay* (like a promissory note), would also be valuable for enforcing the option. As the buyer, you will want your option fee to be as little as possible (or only pay a security deposit), giving you less of a risk.

Wendy's Wisdom

Security Deposit money is always better than option money as far as the buyer's perspective. Why? A security deposit is refundable, but an option fee is not.

Sales Contract

The *Sales Contract* or *Purchase Agreement* is the document that covers the details of the purchase of your home. It includes the purchase price and what non-permanent features of the home are included in the purchase; such as the appliances, furnishings or the gorgeous 1965 Mustang convertible in the garage. It specifies how the home is to be paid for at the end of the option time period; either a mortgage or cash sale. Okay, it probably won't be cash so don't get too worried! The Sales Contract also specifies all of the other terms and conditions of the actual sale. For instance, how the property taxes will be prorated, whether the buyer will have a home inspection, etc. In this case, it is a rent-to-own transaction so the Purchase Agreement also notes that it is part of the Option to Purchase Agreement; thereby binding them together.

Note from Wendy – Buyers and sellers can sometimes get very hung up on one particular item in the house. For the buyers, it could be the one thing that really sold them on the house, even though it's not attached, such as a wood burning stove or pool table. For the sellers, it could be the one thing they absolutely want to take with them. It's amazing how intense negotiations can be over this one particular item, sometimes even breaking the deal. We're talking about a house worth a couple of hundred thousand dollars and the buyers and sellers are hung up on an item worth maybe $600! Remember to keep it all in perspective.

The Terms

In addition to the paperwork, which defines the details of the transaction, there are some terms of the agreements that are quite particular to rent-to-own transactions. In addition to being unique, they are extremely important. The terms cover the different financial aspects of the transaction, which can greatly affect YOUR bottom line.

In Chapter 11 - "Key Points to Negotiate – Not All Deals are Created Equal", we will cover how you can negotiate these terms to make the deal better for you. They are:

Monthly Option Credit- As we mentioned, this is a portion of the monthly rent credited towards the purchase price ONLY if the tenant-buyer exercises the option to purchase. This credit is in no way mandatory, but can be very helpful to the buyer when it comes time to purchase. As the buyer, you will want to get as much in option credit as possible.

Monthly Rent Amount- Typically, rents are priced at market rent or a little bit more on a rent-to-own transaction, however, this amount can always be negotiated to make it better for you.

End Purchase Price- The amount the buyer will pay for the home once he exercises the right to purchase. This final amount will determine the buyer's new mortgage payments. Here are some factors you should consider when deciding what to offer for the house.

- **It's a rent-to-own** - Some rent-to-own sales may command a slightly higher purchase price; possibly as much as 5 to 10% more, depending on the strength of the real estate market in that area. As the buyer, of course, you don't want to pay more than market value; you really want to get a deal on your new home.

- **Items that are included in the sale** - Items such as appliances, furnishings, pool tables and other properties all have monetary value. If you include the refrigerator, stove, dishwasher, washer and dryer in the purchase, you can be adding thousands of dollars worth of value. Don't overlook the value of these items when determining the purchase price you will be offering.

- **Who will make repairs** - Who will be responsible for repairs during the rental period? Every repair costs money. If the home ends up needing a big-ticket item such as a roof or a furnace, it will be expensive. This is a point you can negotiate with the seller. This will be discussed in detail later in the book.

- **Closing costs** - The costs associated with the sale of the home, such as title insurance, mortgage origination or points, payment to the closing agent, etc. can be quite expensive. It is fairly common to include part of these costs in the mortgage to help reduce the amount of money the buyer has to pay out-of-pocket at the closing. When you talk to a lender (before you rent-to-own), get an estimate on how much you'll need to close on the home. See if any of these costs are negotiable.

- **Homeowner's Association (HOA) or yearly fees -**
  Lawn service, home security systems, etc. are all monthly
  and yearly maintenance fees and dues associated with the
  home. Other examples of these are pool service, lawn
  sprinkler maintenance and even country club fees. Many
  homes won't have these or at least not all of them.
  Assigning responsibility for payment of these fees should
  be part of the negotiations.

Example: Let's take a look at a sample transaction to help
you understand the process.

John and Joan Homebuyers were told by their loan officer
that they couldn't qualify for a mortgage. "You must improve your
credit score first." They live in a "down" real estate market and
know that now is a good time to buy. They have always dreamed of
home ownership and want a home NOW. They enlist the help of
Sally Agent, a local Realtor®, who understands how to do rent-to-
own home transactions.

From talking with their loan officer, John and Joan have
determined that once they qualify for a mortgage, they can afford the
payments on a $220,000 home. So they begin to look in that price
range. Alan and Ashley Homeseller live in the same market. A few
months ago, Alan received a promotion at work that requires them to
relocate to another city. Alan and Ashley know the real estate
market is down, but they have no choice but to sell their home now.
They have it listed with Realtor® Thomas Broker (and yes, I do go
to great lengths to come up with these names).

Alan and Ashley have had their home listed for 4 months at
$225,000 without any offers. The need to get their home sold is
getting urgent. Their agent, Thomas, recommends Alan and Ashley
reduce the asking price to $215,000. After Thomas explains to them

how it works, Alan and Ashley agree to add the rent-to-own to their listing.

Soon, Sally Agent shows the house to John and Joan, who decide to make an offer on it. Their initial offer is $205,000 for the purchase price. They agree to the asking rent amount of $1,400 per month and ask for a $500 per month option credit. For their option fee, John and Joan offer 1%, or $2,050, and a $250 security deposit. They also ask that all appliances in the house (refrigerator, stove, dishwasher, washer and dryer) be included. After receiving the offer through Thomas, Alan and Ashley make a counter-offer of $210,000 for the purchase price, $200 per month option credit and an option fee of 2.5%, or $5,250, with a $750 security deposit. They agree to all of the appliances, except for the refrigerator which is brand new and they want to take it with them.

Getting closer to an agreement, John and Joan counter back accepting the $210,000 purchase price, but ask for a $350 per month option credit and an option fee of 2%, or $4,200, with a $500 security deposit. They agree to let Alan and Ashley take the refrigerator, but they ask for an 18-month lease and option period instead of 12 months to give them extra time to get their credit in order. (By the way, most tenant-buyers will require 18 months or longer. Very few buyers can repair their credit in less time with the current mortgage climate. Make sure you ask for enough time. The longer, the better it is for you, even if you don't need it all. If you can get three to five years, I recommend you ask for it.)

Happy to have finally found a new home, John and Joan make plans to move in two weeks. Alan and Ashley are happy to have found buyers for their home and all agree to sign the paperwork in two weeks, giving Alan and Ashley time to move out.

Note from Wendy: At this point, it's a good idea to give an earnest money deposit to the sellers to secure the home. Your agent can assist you with this.

When they meet to finalize the deal, they sign the Lease Agreement, the Option Agreement and the Sales Contract. Because the home was built after 1978, the home will not have lead in the paint. They must still sign a Lead Based Paint Disclosure (this is Federal law), as well as the Seller's Disclosure form (property condition) as mandated in their state. Additionally, as part of a smart practice for rentals, they complete a Property Inventory/Check-in Check-out form (unit condition form), which simply details any issues or problems with the home at time of possession.

Here is a breakdown of the money that John and Joan need to bring the day of the paperwork signing:

Option Fee - $4,200

Security Deposit - $500

First Month's Rent - $1,400

For a total of = $6,100

From this total, any deposit already paid at the time of initial offer in the form of earnest money would be deducted.

Once John and Joan sign the paperwork and give the money to Alan and Ashley, they can move in immediately, only 2 weeks after they reached an agreement!

During the rental period, John and Joan take steps to improve their credit score. They didn't have enough money left to buy a new refrigerator, but were able to get financing on one. They were very careful to make all of the payments when due and pay it off in one year. In addition, they paid off two smaller credit cards. They diligently made all utility and other payments on time.

After 15 months in the home, John and Joan notify Alan and Ashley that they want to purchase the house. From the day they moved in, they took steps toward improving their credit and to work with their loan officer and apply for a mortgage. By making on-time payments and paying off debts, their loan officer is able to get them approved for the mortgage amount they need to buy this home. Home ownership is now within their reach.

How to Get Started

In the next section we'll talk about finding your new home. Reading this book is a great start in the right direction. But you've got to get moving. Unfortunately, reading this book isn't enough. You'll have to actually take the steps to get things going.

We are going to go over lots of things in this book, and you won't be able to do it all at once. I recommend taking it one step at a time, that's the best way. Choose one step to put into action and do it. After you've done that one, choose another and do that. You'll find it's very easy to convert reading this book into action if you break it into small and manageable steps.

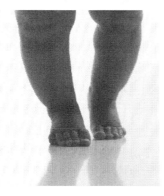

Take baby steps.

PART 2:

HOW TO SEARCH FOR A HOME

Chapter 3

House Hunting Basics

There are many things to consider before deciding on your rent-to-own home, so that you don't end up in a home that you won't meet your needs.

Searching for a new home is an exciting process! Sometimes it can get a little scary, but for the most part it can be a lot of fun. As a real estate agent, I love showing potential homes to buyers. Getting a new home is a process filled with anticipation and dreams of your life in your new space. Homebuyers dream of summer barbeques in the yard, children or pets playing on the lawn, a cozy bedroom to sleep in at night and the prospect of owning something that helps build a financial and personal future.

Before you rush right out and actually hit the streets looking for a home, there are a couple of things you need to take into account. The first is to set and follow a budget. You need to determine how much you can afford. Home ownership is a dream and we don't want it to become a financial nightmare. It is important to work with your lender in advance for a realistic idea of what you can afford and will be able to afford at the end of the term of your agreement.

Setting a Budget – How Much House Can You Afford

The first step is talking with a mortgage broker. Even if you can't get approved for a mortgage right now, he can still help you determine how much you can get approved for later. He has formulas that calculate the maximum amount you can qualify for in a mortgage. These formulas are based on your income and debts. Most mortgage lenders use a debt-to-income ratio (DTI) of 28/36 and FHA limits are typically 31/43. Let me explain what those numbers mean. (If you are looking for a lender, you can go to my website www.WendyPatton.com, click on the Rent-to-Own link, then click whether you are a buyer, seller, investor or real estate agent, and then click on Find a Mortgage Lender).

The first number in the debt-to-income ratio (DTI), 28 (or 31 for FHA) is called the *front ratio*. The front ratio is the percentage of income that can count towards housing costs, or PITI, which are Principal, Interest, Taxes and Insurance. That means that 28% (or 31% for FHA) of your *gross income* (before taxes are taken out) can count towards these costs.

The second number, 36 (or 43 for FHA) is called the *back ratio*. The back ratio includes the amounts from the front ratio (PITI) plus any other recurring debt payments, such as car loans, credit cards, student loans, child support, alimony or legal judgments. This does not count things like groceries, utilities and so forth. Again, this means that 36% (or 43% for FHA) of your gross income can count towards these costs.

Let's take a look at an example. Suppose your annual household income is $60,000 per year. You divide that amount by 12 months, which equals $5,000 per month (before taxes). Here is how we calculate DTI.

Front Ratio

$5,000 gross monthly income X .28 (the front ratio) = $1,400

$5,000 gross monthly income X .31 (FHA front ratio) = $1,550

Back Ratio

$5,000 gross monthly income X .36 (the back ratio) = $1,800

$5,000 gross monthly income X .43 (FHA back ratio) = $2,150

What do these numbers mean? For a non-FHA loan with $60,000 per year gross income, a home buyer can afford (and thus qualify for) $1,400 per month for mortgage payments, including Principal, Interest, Taxes and Insurance (PITI). Additionally it means that the total monthly debt payments can be $1,800 per month or an extra $400 per month over the cost of housing for things like car loans, credit cards and so on. For an FHA loan, a borrower could afford $1,550 per month for housing and a total of $2,150 for all debts.

This part is something you can easily calculate on your own. Just take your annual gross income and multiply it by .28 and .36. But here is where the calculations get tricky and a mortgage broker would be valuable. With the $60,000 per year income, our front end ratio is $1,400 per month, which covers PITI. How much house does that actually buy?

This will depend on several factors. It will depend on the interest rate for the loan, the property tax rate for your area and the price of homeowner's insurance.

Wendy's Wisdom

Don't worry about trying to muddle through these numbers yourself. Get help from a mortgage broker. Even if you are a whiz at numbers and want to do it yourself, you'll still need a mortgage broker to assist you because he will process your loan application. Ask friends or family members for the name of their lender.

Property taxes, interest rates and insurance will all vary. They vary from person to person, state to state, city to city, all the way down to neighborhood by neighborhood. For example, a person buying a home in my beloved state of Michigan will pay entirely different property taxes and insurance than a person buying a home in Florida. Not only that, but the property taxes in a city like Orlando may be vastly different from the property taxes in a city like Dallas, Texas.

Homeowner's insurance varies neighborhood by neighborhood and is based on assorted factors like crime, proximity to fire stations, how prone the area is to natural disasters and so forth.

Interest rates will also vary, but these usually vary based on a buyer's credit score and some other factors the mortgage industry doesn't want us to ever know (probably things like the CEO wants to buy a new Mercedes this month).

Not even a mortgage broker can figure all of that out exactly down to the last dollar. Typically, they use best estimates based on your area. Let's go back to the question of how much house will $1,400 per month buy?

I'm going to assume the following:

1. The interest rate will be 5.5%

2. Property taxes will be $3,000 per year (based on national averages)

3. Homeowners insurance will be $900 per year (based on national averages, however, areas prone to hurricanes, earthquakes, forest fires and flooding may be higher)

4. The home buyer has a $5,000 down payment (approximately 3%)

The answer to our question, based on all of these assumptions, is that a $1,400 per month payment would equal a purchase price of about $175,000. But let's play with the numbers a little bit. Suppose instead of a 3% down payment, you accumulate a 6% down payment from a 2% option fee, and another 4% in option credits. Suppose also, that instead of a 5.5% interest rate, the buyer gets a 5% interest rate due to the larger down payment and increased credit score. What would that do to the numbers? Would you believe that the buyer could afford $190,000 instead of $175,000? That's a pretty big difference.

Now, you'll recall there was also a back ratio of $1,800 in this example. That means after the $1,400 per month housing payment, the buyer can afford another $400 for recurring monthly debts like car payments, student loans, credit cards and so forth. If you have more than that amount in extra payments, you would be able to afford less home. Instead of $400 per month, let's say our buyer has $500 per month in additional debts. How much does that cost them? Instead of being able to buy a $175,000 home they would only be able to buy a $159,000 home.

Wendy's Wisdom

When buying using a rent-to-own sale, you have time to pay off some debts. In this case, just paying off a $25/ month debt would allow our buyer to obtain an additional $4,000 in purchasing power.

Okay, hopefully you've talked with a mortgage broker by now and he has helped determine the maximum amount of a mortgage you can qualify for. Something to keep in mind is that this amount is the maximum amount. It doesn't necessarily mean that you should try to buy a home for that much money. You may very well want to buy something for less than that. Remember, you want homeownership to be a dream, not a nightmare.

Let's take a look at our example buyer with the $60,000 per year gross income. We'll set a monthly budget and determine how affordable this house payment is. I'm going to assume our buyer is married with two children and lives in Michigan and will use the tax rate for that state. The federal tax bracket for our buyer's income is 15%, plus we deduct Social Security, Medicare and the state tax rate (which is extremely confusing and there is no need to go into the calculations here) to get a result of $4,048 per month after taxes. After we deduct the $1,800 per month for housing costs and other debts, we have a balance of $2,248 left for everything else.

Let's take a look at our buyer's monthly budget:

After tax monthly income	$4,048
Housing costs	-1,400
Other debts	-$400
Retirement savings	-$250
Groceries	-$650
Utilities (water, gas, electric)	-$240
Gasoline	-$300
Cellular phone and regular phone	-$150
Cable TV/Satellite & Internet Service	-$125
Eating out and other entertainment	-$250
Clothes and other misc. expenses	-$150
Balance	**$133**

Wendy's Wisdom

Be conservative and spend less than you can afford. This will help keep you out of trouble in the future.

As you can see, on a relatively modest budget there isn't too much left over. What happens if the car needs repairs, or you have to replace a water heater or something like that? How will you pay for your vacation? How will you pay for your kids' clothes, etc.? Your budget is very tight.

This is why you need to take a realistic look at your own monthly budget. Save your receipts for the next couple of months and determine how much some things cost you. How much are you spending on gas, groceries, eating out and so forth? Work out a budget that you and your family can not only afford, but will be happy with. As part of being a homeowner you may need to make some sacrifices, like eating out a little less often or sneaking snacks into the movie theater instead of buying $12 candy bars for your children (I'm not saying I ever did this☺), but you don't want to make so many sacrifices that you are miserable.

You definitely want to have something left over each month so you can save for contingencies, vacations or the like. While it's important to plan for contingencies, you certainly can't plan for every inevitability. If you tried to do that you might never take the step to home ownership. You want to set a realistic budget, not an overly optimistic budget and not an overly pessimistic budget. This is where you need to consider whether you can <u>really</u> afford that much house payment. Should you buy a less expensive home so your payment is lower?

Wendy's Wisdom

Setting a manageable family budget is an important step when buying a home. You don't want to get in over your head. If you do, the dream of homeownership will quickly turn into a difficult situation. If you set a realistic budget, you will find that you are comfortably able to enjoy your new home.

Important Features

Now that you've set a budget and know how much home you can afford, it's time to start thinking about what features you want and need in a home. Consider your needs, not just now, but also for the next few years. For example, if you don't have any children now but plan on having some over the next few years, a one-bedroom cottage probably won't be a good choice for you. On the other hand, if you have five kids, a home with one bathroom is just not practical. Take a look at your situation. If you have owned a home before it will be easier for you to determine your needs than if this is your first home.

It is important, however, to get an idea of your needs before you go out looking at homes so you aren't just floundering around. It's okay to refine your needs as you are looking at homes and think more about your future home, but decide on your basic must-haves beforehand.

Here are some basic needs you'll want to consider:

1. How many bedrooms?

2. Do you need a garage?

3. Do you need a basement or other structure for storage, like a shed (of course, you don't want a basement in Florida)?

4. How big do the bedrooms need to be (if you have two children sharing a bedroom, do you need something larger for them)?

5. How many bathrooms will be needed?

6. How big of a yard and landscaping are you willing to care for?

Think also about the specifics of your own situation. Will you have an elderly parent living with you? If you or a family member is physically disabled, can the home be two stories or should it only have one? If you have small children, do you need a fenced in yard? It's impossible to cover every particular situation, but you know better than anyone what applies to the needs of your family.

Once you have established your basic *needs* for a home, it's time to think about features you *want*. There is definitely a difference between *needs* and *wants*. *Needs* are things that, if they aren't met, they won't make the home functional for you or your family. *Wants* are things you would like to have, but if you don't have them, you can function without them. Wants are often items that may put you over your budgeted price.

For example, if you want a house that is waterfront, you should expect to pay a price premium for that. If that price premium stretches the budget we talked about earlier, you need to decide both whether you can afford it and how important that feature is to you.

Wendy's Wisdom

If you are too broke to enjoy it, there isn't much point in buying a waterfront home or a house on ten acres of land. Stay within your budget when you think about features you want.

Here are some features that are usually considered wants:
1. Home office
2. Extra bathrooms
3. Master suite
4. Garage
5. Basement
6. Home theater
7. Island kitchen
8. Fireplace
9. Waterfront or other exceptional lot feature

You'll notice that home offices and basements appear both in the wants list and in the needs list. Depending on your circumstances, they could be either. For example, if you run your own business and work out of your home, a home office is probably a need for you, not a want.

Location Factors

As they say in real estate, the three most important things to consider when buying a home is location, location, location. Now that we've established what you *need* and *want* in a home, you need to decide *where* to look for a home.

1. **School District**: There are some important components to location when making this decision. If you have children, one of the big ones is the school district. If your children are already in school, you need to decide if you want to stay in the same school district so they don't have to change. If they aren't yet in school, you want to consider what school district you prefer, and specifically what schools in the district you want them to attend. Historically, homes in good school districts appreciate better and hold their value better than equivalent homes with poorer quality schools. This makes school selection not just an important investment in your children, but also an important investment in your home.

2. **Work**: Another important location factor to consider is proximity to work. Given the uncertainty of the cost of gasoline, commuting costs are definitely worth factoring in. It's also important to factor in the amount of time your commute takes. If you live an hour away from where you work, not only are the gas costs going to be enormous, but that means two hours per day of driving, which is a lot of extra time away from home.

3. **Lifestyle**: Amenities are also important when deciding on location. How close do you want to be to the grocery store, your favorite restaurants and your favorite entertainment locations? Long travel times to get to these locations is not just inconvenient, but adds to gas costs too. In some cases, if you are trying to cut down on dining out to save money, you might want to move just a bit farther away from your favorite restaurants so you are less likely to frequent them.

4. **Safety**: The last location factor to take into account is crime. For the sake of the safety of you and your family, the lower the crime rates, the better. It will also affect the long-term value of your home. If you live in a high crime area, appreciation rates will be slower and in a down market, your home will decline in value faster. Larger cities tend to have higher crime rates than small towns, so you can't compare the crime rate in San Francisco, California to Cheboygan, Michigan. However, many cities have good and bad neighborhoods. As a general rule, the better the neighborhood, the better off you are.

In summary, you want a house that is in the best school district, a five minute or less commute to work, close to all of the best amenities and in a zero crime neighborhood. If you find one, let me know because I'm not sure they really exist. Obviously, when you add all of these factors together, selecting the location for your home is a series of compromises. You want good schools, but you don't want that to put you an hour away from work. You want to be close to amenities that are important to you, but not too close if it means you have to settle for a high crime neighborhood, and so on.

Resale Value

When you look for a home, it's also a good idea to take into consideration how easily you will be able to resell the home.

"What?" you say. "Wendy, that's crazy. I haven't even bought the home and you're telling me I need to think about selling it?"

I know it sounds funny, but think about this. The average family only lives in a home for 5 to 7 years. This means that in most cases, you will be selling the home that you're buying within 5-7 years. Since the odds are that you'll be selling it, it is wise to think about how sellable the home is when you buy it.

Take into consideration the location factors we just talked about. If you buy a home in a really bad neighborhood, you are going to have more trouble selling it than if it's in a good neighborhood or has good schools, and so forth.

Consider the house itself. Does the house have curb appeal? If not, can you give it curb appeal? Some homes are just ugly, but some can be saved with some elbow grease and a little bit of money. You'll encounter this yourself when you are out looking for homes. Think about how a home's appearance affects you. If you don't like it, odds are most other buyers won't either.

Factor in the floor plan and the interior functionality. Real estate agents have a term called "functionally obsolete". That means that the home just doesn't work. Things like having to walk through one bedroom to get to another bedroom, or a bathroom that was added on as an afterthought and you have to duck your head to get through the doorway are the types of things that make a home functionally obsolete. This doesn't mean it's not usable; it's just not as desirable.

Wendy's Wisdom

A good rule to keep in mind is that if you don't like the home, most other buyers won't either. Always consider resale when you are buying real estate.

With all of that said, however, remember that there can be great opportunity in homes like these. With these types of homes you have to have imagination and be able to visualize the outcome.

If you can do that, you can imagine whether the home is salvageable or if it's better to move on to the next one.

If you are the type of person who likes to take a diamond in the rough and turn it into a thing of beauty, you can build some equity in a rent-to-own home. Most homeowners selling ugly or functionally obsolete homes know that their home needs help. As part of your negotiations, you can request option credits for repairs and improvements. For example, if an improvement only costs you $800 in materials, but would cost the homeowner $3,000 to have the work done, you can negotiate an option credit for $3,000 or more and do the work yourself. This gives you $2,200 in *equity*. I'll go into more detail regarding this later.

The Emotions of Home Buying

Buying a home is almost always an emotion-based process. Once you find a home you like, you become emotionally attached to it. Emotional attachment can cause you to make unwise decisions when making an offer, handling negotiations, and so forth. Once you've fallen in love with a house and visualized it being your home, you'll start to do WHATEVER it takes to make sure it becomes your home.

This is about the worst possible way to buy a home, but also may be the best possible home for you. You do want to fall in love with your new home, but you also want to be careful.

You can literally cost yourself thousands of dollars, if not tens of thousands of dollars, by being too emotionally attached. Instead of letting emotions rule the game, try to include some common sense in the buying process. Real estate investors have a saying that goes, "Don't fall in love with the house, fall in love with the deal." This is easier for an investor as he won't live there, but you should be aware of this, and use your head.

Having said that, I realize that you will always have some emotional attachment to your house. You need to like it. Your goal is to strike a balance between liking the house and using common sense to tell you whether you are sacrificing too much to try to get the house. If you find you have to make lots and lots of compromises to get a house, stop yourself and ask, "Is this really worth it?"

The following is a story that illustrates the emotions of home buying.

A real estate agent I know told me that he was showing rental homes to a couple with five children. They were looking for a newer home with at least four bedrooms, a basement, a two-car garage and a short commute time to work. There were several homes to choose from in their price range:

House #1 was a builder's model and had never been lived in. It was completely empty with no furnishings, but the appliances were included. This home had seen numerous walk-throughs and the carpet was a little dirty, the landscaping wasn't in very good shape and the basement floor had many hairline cracks in the concrete. In short, despite being brand new, the home didn't show very well and it had the highest rental rate. However, it was very large in size and met all of their needs, including a short commute time.

House #2 was about five years old and was almost the same size as the builder's model. It had a ton of built-in storage in the garage, as well as a very open floor plan. As a bonus, it had a fifth room in the basement that could be used as a bedroom, which gave all of the kids their own rooms. Unfortunately, this home didn't show all that well either. The owners were in the process of moving out, so there were only odds and ends strewn about the home and there were two pipes dripping in the basement over the laundry area. The rental rate was $100 per month less than the builder's model and the commute time was about the same.

House #3 was the smallest. It still had the four bedrooms, garage and basement, but was clearly smaller than the other two and was about ten years old. It was also the farthest away, adding 15 minutes commute time each way. The rental rate was $25 per month more than the second home, even though the neighborhood wasn't any better. This home was beautifully staged (staging is when a home is decorated or laid out for maximum appeal, kind of like Martha Stewart was living in the house), all of the furnishings were present and were well laid out. The dining room table was set with fine china. The master bedroom had a nicely coordinated bedroom set. None of the furnishings were included with the rental, but it gave the family a chance to visualize living in the home and picture in their mind where they would put their own things.

Guess which house the couple chose? You guessed it: House #3. Despite the fact that it was the farthest away and the smallest home, they liked what they saw and felt. If you took away the home staging that had been done, there was absolutely nothing about this home that was better than the other two. In fact, it was inferior in pretty much every way, but it LOOKED GOOD! The couple became emotionally attached to the home and chose it.

This is a perfect example of where common sense would have been useful. The couple chose the house that was the worst option for meeting their needs, but they fell in love with it.

While you are looking at homes and once you make an offer on a home, there are some questions you should be asking yourself to help keep common sense involved in the decision making process:

1. Does the home work for you and does it meet your NEEDS?

   Remember the difference between *wants* and *needs?*

2. Do the numbers work for you?

   Can you really afford this home?

3. What sacrifices are you making to get this home?

   It helps to think specifically about what you might be giving up for this particular home.

4. Will the home meet your needs for the near future?

   Will your family be growing? Are the kids going away to college?

   Will you still want to mow that big back yard in a few years?

If you know that you are the type of person who easily becomes emotional in your decision making process, it might be a good idea to carry a note card with these four questions on it to remind you while you are looking!

Wendy's Wisdom

Remember to strike a balance between emotions and common sense in your home buying process. It will help you enjoy your home that much more once you actually move in.

One big advantage to buying a home as a rent-to-own is that you get to live in the home for a while before you have to make a decision about buying it. This means that if you became overly emotional during the decision making process, common sense will have a chance to kick in while you are living there. However, you do need to keep in mind that if you choose not to buy the home, you will be forfeiting your option fee.

Now that we've gone over the basics of house hunting, we'll take a look at how you can use a real estate agent to help you in your search. You might be surprised to know that in most cases, real estate agents are FREE for home buyers.

Chapter 4

Using a Realtor®

A good real estate agent will work hard for you to help you find and rent-to-own the home that is best for you and your family.

Let's start with how to pronounce this word. It is not "real-a-tor," it is "real-tor". There are two syllables in Realtor®, but most people pronounce it with three. All Realtors® are real estate agents, but not all real estate agents are Realtors®. In order to be a Realtor®, you need to belong to the National Association of Realtors® (NAR). Realtors® take mandatory training every year and are required to adhere to a *code of ethics*. I use the terms Realtor® and real estate agent interchangeably throughout this book, but it is important to understand that there can be a difference. If you are a real estate agent, there is a section at the end of this book just for you.

Most of you reading this are probably not yet working with a real estate agent because many real estate agents will tell you that if you can't get approved for financing, they can't help you. Don't worry! There are real estate agents out there who know how to do rent-to-own transactions and will be able to help you find your new home. If you need to find a real estate agent in your area, please email my office at Refer@WendyPatton.com and I will help you find an agent knowledgeable and experienced in rent-to-own transactions in your area.

If you are trying to decide whether or not to work with an agent, this chapter should help you. In my opinion, the pros of working with a real estate agent definitely outweigh the cons. I will go over both sides so you can make the decision for yourself.

Buyer's Agent Versus Listing Agent

It is important to understand that there are typically two types of agents in a real estate transaction: the *listing agent* and the *buyer's agent*. However, two agents are not required. Sometimes the listing agent will handle *both* sides of the transaction. The *listing agent* is the agent who is marketing the home for sale; he is listing it *for the seller* and is also called a *seller's agent* (the *buyer's agent*, if there is one, *represents the buyer* in the transaction).

When you are working with a particular real estate agent, be it a buyer's agent or a listing agent, he should have you sign an *Agency Disclosure*. This disclosure tells you what your agent's role in the transaction is; whether it is as a *listing agent*, a *buyer's agent* or even a *transaction coordinator or dual agent*. A transaction coordinator, in most cases, was a listing agent who is now handling both sides of the transaction which changed his role and in turn, his responsibilities. Remember that the listing agent, or seller's agent, has responsibilities to look out for the seller's best interests. The buyer's agent looks out for the buyer's best interests. This is extremely important throughout the process, especially during negotiations. If you, as a buyer, call about a house from the sign, and that agent (which is the listing agent) shows you the house, he will be representing and looking out for the seller's interests - not yours. He remains the seller's agent. That is why I highly recommend always working with a buyer's agent who will act on your behalf.

Each state has its own definition of how agents represent clients. Your agent will be able to explain the differences and the responsibilities each has to his clients.

A listing agent will have fiduciary responsibility to the seller. A buyer's agent will have fiduciary responsibility to you, the buyer. A transaction coordinator will oversee the transaction, but will not have a fiduciary responsibility to *either* the buyer or seller.

Let's look at an example of how this works. Let's say that Annie Agent is a listing agent and, therefore, has fiduciary responsibility to the seller, Sam Seller. Sam Seller tells Annie Agent that he urgently needs to sell his home and that he would be willing to take an offer for significantly less than the current asking price. You and your family have been through the house and love it, but feel it is over-priced. You move on, thinking you cannot afford it. The information that Sam told Annie would have been very useful to you as a buyer wouldn't it? Because Annie Agent has the *fiduciary responsibility* to Sam Seller, she is not supposed to reveal information that the seller tells her; either to a buyer's agent or to you, the buyer. The same would go for an agent whose fiduciary responsibility is to you. If you told your agent that you loved a particular home so much you would pay full price to get it, don't you think the seller would want to know this? A buyer's agent is not supposed to reveal what you told him - not to the listing agent nor to the seller. Most agents will keep this information confidential.

Now, as a potential homebuyer, you are not obligated to work with either the listing agent or a buyer's agent. It is your choice. For example, if you drive by a home for sale that is listed by a Realtor®, you have the option of either contacting the listing agent directly to see the home or contacting a buyer's agent and have him show you the home. Let's take a look at the pros and cons of working with a Realtor®.

Note from Wendy: All Realtors® have an ethical responsibility to act fairly to ALL parties in a real estate transaction.

If you are the type of buyer who likes to do research on your own, you might find a listing that is advertised as a rent-to-own. This is just what you are looking for. You give the agent a call and ask to see the house, right? It depends on your perspective after reading the above information.

If you choose not to work with a real estate agent or want to expand your options for choices, the next chapter is for you. I will explain how to find rent-to-own sellers who are not listing their home as rent-to-own. Even if you are working with a real estate agent, the next chapter will be useful. Share it with your real estate agent. Many sellers out there, even ones listed in the MLS, may not know about rent-to-own, but will happily consider it to get their home sold. You just need to find them.

Pros for Working with a Realtor®

They're FREE!

No, you didn't read that wrong, I said free! In MOST cases, real estate agents are paid by the seller, not the buyer, as part of the agreement they have with the seller.

Here is a quick explanation of how it works. When a real estate agent agrees to list a home for a seller, he has a commission agreement, meaning that if the home is sold while the real estate agent has it listed; the seller will pay a commission to that agent's brokerage. The brokerage will then pay the listing agent their portion of that commission. This commission covers the selling and buying sides of the transaction. These commissions are typically split between both agents, if there are two. If there is no buyer's agent and the listing Realtor® covers both sides of the transaction, they get to keep all of the commission. This is referred to as "double dipping".

What this means to you is that the seller has already agreed to pay a commission to the buyer's agent before you even entered the picture. It doesn't mean that if you don't use an agent that commission won't get paid, it will all just go to the listing agent's brokerage. So there isn't any reason for you <u>not</u> to use a buyer's agent to help you find your home.

In some cases, if the seller is going the "For Sale by Owner" route, he may not be willing to pay a commission. If that were the case and you wanted to use a buyer's agent, you might have to pay that agent's brokerage yourself. Just to clarify, a real estate agent only gets paid by his brokerage. They cannot accept a fee directly for their services. It must be paid to them through their broker. The buyer or seller would never pay the agent directly, but would pay the brokerage and the brokerage pays the agent their portion.

According to the National Association of Realtor's® "2007 Profile of Home Buyers and Sellers", 81 percent of home buyers and 84 percent sellers used a real estate professional, which comparable to 2007. That means you are far more likely to find your rent-to-own home listed with a real estate agent than not.

Multiple Listing Service (MLS)

The MLS is the single greatest real estate marketing tool in existence. Any seller with a home listed through a Realtor® should have the home listed in the MLS. This is where your agent, the buyer's agent, will go to find your home.

If you search for homes on the Internet on sites like Realtor.com, Yahoo!® Real Estate, Zillow or Trulia, you are actually seeing homes that are listed on the MLS. Those sites are fed by the MLS. If you are looking at listings for homes on a particular real estate agent's website, you are also looking at homes that are fed from the MLS. If you look at the home magazine publications that have homes for sale with different real estate agents, you are seeing homes that are in the MLS. If you look at the newspaper and see homes for sale with a real estate agent, you are seeing homes that are listed in the MLS.

Are you starting to get a sense of what an incredible marketing tool the MLS is? Simply put, if you want to find a home, the MLS is the place to look, and the MLS is controlled by real estate agents.

Assistance with Paperwork

Yes, there is a lot of paperwork associated with buying your home, whether it is as a rent-to-own or a traditional sale. There is more paperwork with a rent-to-own than a conventional sale. Each state, and even some municipalities, has specific requirements for what paperwork and contracts must be part of a real estate transaction. Real estate agents will know which clauses you should add to my contracts for your area.

Wendy's Wisdom

Work with a real estate agent to handle the paperwork. If you are buying from a "For Sale by Owner" and are not using a buyer's agent, you should make use of an attorney to assist you.
I don't recommend creating the paperwork on your own.

There can be quite a bit of paperwork associated with buying your home. If you try to do it all yourself, it might seem overwhelming!

I will go into detail about essential rent-to-own contracts that need to be included in your transaction and where to get these forms in later chapters.

In addition to making sure you have completed all of the necessary paperwork, a real estate agent can help you to make sure that the paperwork you complete gives you the protection you need. A common mistake people make is thinking all contracts are created equal. This is most often NOT TRUE. Making sure you have all of the proper terms and conditions in your contracts is absolutely critical.

For example, would you think it was possible for a seller to make you pay for their son's braces? If it is in the contract, you didn't notice it and signed the contract, guess what—you will be financing their son's smile.

The point I'm trying to make is that just about any clause that appears in a real estate contract can be enforceable, so it is important that you have help with your contracts. I would strongly suggest that if you don't use a real estate agent, you at least hire a real estate attorney for help with your contracts. If you want to save a ton on real estate attorney fees, use my forms and have a Pre-Paid Legal attorney review them at *no charge*. Go to www.GotLegalPlans.com for more information. These legal plans start at just $16.00 per month on a month-to-month basis, with no annual contract required.

Seriously though, the average seller knows very little about contracts and will almost always rely on whatever contracts their agent provides. You will want to provide the contracts for the rent-to-own deal. This way they are set up in your favor. I call these "pro-buyer" contracts. They are included in the companion course to this book, which is available through my website bookstore at www.WendyPatton.com.

Wendy's Wisdom

Not all contracts are created equal! Make sure you use the right contracts to protect yourself in the purchase of your home. Even if your real estate agent wants to use his state approved contract (and he will), he can use the pro-buyer clauses in my contracts to enhance his contracts to favor you.

Comparables (Comps)

Comparables are an analysis of similar, nearby properties which are "compared" to determine the value of a home. Real estate agents can provide you with "comps" to help you understand what a home is worth.

Sellers use comps to determine how much they should ask for their home. Buyers use them to determine if the home they want to buy is priced fairly. In some cases you, as a buyer, may need to pay a price premium for a rent-to-own home. You are not always in the driver's seat when you buy a rent-to-own home. This will depend, to some extent, on how well the seller understands the value of selling his home as a rent-to-own. It will also depend on your real estate market. If you are living in a buyer's market, you are less likely to have to pay a premium than in a seller's market. I will talk more about this in Chapter 11 – "Key Points to Negotiate".

A good real estate agent has some "tricks up his sleeve" from past experience that can help you out tremendously during the negotiation period.

Let's face it, these days most of us like to do some research on our own using the Internet. It's a great place to start when looking for your rent-to-own home. While it's a great place to start, it doesn't make you an expert on home buying. Why would you want to be? If you were going to buy a car, would you go out and learn how to build it first or go to work for a car dealership just to buy the car? Of course not.

A good real estate agent knows his market: the neighborhoods, the laws, the contracts and so forth. He is a trained professional in the business of buying and selling homes. An experienced real estate agent has a knowledge base that you as a homebuyer will need for your home purchase. He can guide you through the entire buying process.

Objective Negotiations

Having a real estate agent on your side will help keep the emotion out of the negotiations. Here's an example: Let's say you were buying a rent-to-own home for $150,000. If your real estate agent is helping you with negotiations, he might for example, be able to negotiate a $500 per month option credit (by the way, I have sometimes negotiated as much as the entire month's rent as option credits – so this amount is very feasible). Over an 18-month option period, that saves you $9,000! If you were paying your real estate agent a 3% commission, that would cost you $4,500. With just this one negotiated term, the real estate agent has earned DOUBLE their commission in savings for you!

Could you negotiate these terms yourself? Certainly, but be honest with yourself – how experienced are you at negotiating terms of a home purchase?

Wendy's Wisdom

In rare cases, you may need to pay your buyer's agent instead of the seller paying it. A good agent will earn his commission many times over through the benefits he brings to you.

Cons of Working with a Realtor®

Of course, working with a real estate agent isn't always wine and roses. Sometimes there are disadvantages, too.

Commission

In the last section, I said that real estate agents are free for buyers to work with. Most of the time, this is true. In some cases, however, if the seller isn't paying the full commission, you would need to pay your buyer's agent. This is something you will know up front before you start to work with a real estate agent.

While this would cost you money, a good agent can save you the cost of his commission and more in the benefits he brings to you, such as assistance with paperwork and access to the MLS. An experienced real estate agent can easily earn his commission in negotiations alone. There are many terms to negotiate in a rent-to-own, which we'll cover in Chapter 11.

Not All Agents are Created Equal

There are some agents out there who are much less interested in the quality of service they give you than in getting their commission. These are the types of agents who never get referrals from satisfied customers, with good reason. Most of their customers are not satisfied.

Many agents are not informed about rent-to-own transactions and stay away from them. They feel they may not get their entire commission. However, they do get their total commission; partial commission up front and the remainder at the final closing. When agents place their need for commission before their desire to satisfy your needs, they may push you into poor decisions. Such an agent may negotiate weakly to take no chances at losing the deal. He may recommend paying too high of a purchase price or option fee, not ask for the most appropriate term, and so forth. Fortunately, many real estate agents are starting to realize that renting-to-own is an important option for their clients and they need to learn how to do them correctly.

Getting Them On Board

If you have already been turned down for a mortgage at this time and an agent has told you he can't help you, he doesn't understand creative buying techniques such as rent-to-own. If there is a particular agent that you know you want to work with, but he isn't educated in rent-to-own transactions, you'll need to get him on board. Rather than try to teach him yourself, give him a copy of this book. In the end he'll thank you for it because it will make it much easier for him to earn a living in down real estate markets (or even up markets). He will be able to help other buyers as well. Many buyers today need to use a rent-to-own transaction.

By getting him on board, you'll now be speaking the same language with each other when it comes to rent-to-owns. This is important as he assists you through the process of buying your rent-to-own home. Remember, if you don't have an agent who can help you with rent-to-own, I can find one in your area. Just email my office at Refer@WendyPatton.com.

Chapter 5

Finding Motivated Sellers

Needing a larger home is just one reason why a seller would be

very motivated to do a rent-to-own.

In this chapter, I will cover my favorite and the easiest ways to find sellers willing to do a rent-to-own sale. Most homes that have potential for a rent-to-own are not marketed as rent-to-owns. In fact, many sellers don't even know about the option of selling by rent-to-own. If you do just a little bit of digging (which your real estate agent can help you with), you can turn up the best rent-to-own homes.

There are many ways to find motivated sellers willing to sell you their home. A motivated seller is the best type of seller when you are looking for a rent-to-own home because this type of seller has an urgency to get their home sold. Motivation equals flexibility.

That urgency means they are more willing to be creative to accomplish their goal.

Unmotivated sellers want to sell their home, but don't have urgency. Instead of getting it sold by doing something like rent-to-own, they are willing to let it sit on the market until the perfect conventional buyer comes along. You probably won't want to bother with this type of seller even if they would consider rent-to-own. He'll probably be too much of a headache. He won't be flexible with his terms; he will want ridiculously high option fees and top dollar.

What Makes a Motivated Seller?

Each seller will have his own reason for being motivated, and not all of them are able to do rent-to-own. The best motivated sellers for rent-to-own are the ones seeking what I call "good debt relief". This usually means that the home they are trying to sell is a payment burden but they aren't generally in financial trouble. Here are some examples of motivated sellers:

- They built a new home and the old one hasn't sold yet

- They purchased a new home and the old one hasn't sold yet

- They recently got married and each had their own home - now they need just one

- They were given a job transfer to a new area and haven't sold their old home yet

- They inherited the property

- They are landlords and are selling a rental property

- They are selling a vacation home, or have retired and moved into their vacation home and are selling their old home

In all of these cases, the seller has essentially moved on or doesn't live in the home they are trying to sell. They, most likely, have a second home. What this means is that the seller is burdened with two homes and two mortgage payments. While he might be able to afford that second payment, nobody wants to make a payment on a home that is sitting empty.

Wendy's Wisdom

The best "motivated sellers" to find for rent-to-owns are those with two homes and two mortgage payments.

Finding Motivated Sellers

My favorite ways to find motivated sellers are in this order:

1. Working with Realtors® / real estate agents

2. The "For Rent" ads

3. Advertising to find them – See Chapter 6

4. Getting sellers to call you – See Chapter 6

5. Distressed builders

6. For Sale By Owners – FSBO's

There are many other ways to find motivated sellers, but these are more than enough for what you will need to find your home.

Working with Realtors®

My favorite way to find leads for sellers is through Realtors®. You can't do this one by yourself because you need a real estate agent to look up these listings in the MLS. Only real estate agents have access to these listings. When you are ready to find a new home, a real estate agent can search on key words like "rent-to-own" or "lease option", etc., but most of the listings that can be bought with a lease option are not listed that way. The listings that come up with these key words are potential homes for you, as well as the ones not listed this way. Most agents don't even know their sellers can do a lease option until another agent calls and uses the script I have for them in Part 6 of this book.

Your agent should consider calling about listings with one or more of these conditions:

1. Homes on the market longer than 120 days

2. Homes in your price range

3. Homes that are NOT REO's – Bank Owned

4. Homes that are NOT short sales or upside down in equity

5. Home is vacant

6. Best if the seller is not behind on any mortgage payments

If you are working with a buyer's agent, buy him this book and have him read Chapters 20, 21, 22 and 23 now. If you aren't working with an agent, here are some tricks to get you a potential rent-to-own seller.

Drive around the area you know you want to live in and look for houses listed for sale. You can often tell which ones might be motivated by noticing that the lawn is overgrown, the sign is weathered or it otherwise appears to be vacant. Look for the listing agent's name and telephone number on the sign. If they are not on the sign, call the office number and ask for "the listing agent" for that address.

Script for Calling a Realtor®

Once you have the agent on the phone,
here is what I usually say:

"Hi _____ (the agent's name), my name is _____ (your name) and I was calling about the home you have listed at _____ (the street address). Is it still available?"

After they say, "Yes it is," I would say,

"Can you tell me more about the home? How much is it and how large is it?"

Listen to see if it is something you would be interested in. If so, follow up with:

"I noticed it has been listed a while"... (Assuming it has been listed for more than four months).

Wait and see what they say without saying anything else. They might say, *"Yes..."* and I would go on to the next question, or they might start to talk more – which is what I am hoping they will do. I want them to start to talk and tell me more. Maybe they will tell me why it has been listed a long time or what the status is. You would be amazed at what others will tell you when you zip it and listen. My next question is:

"Well, I wondered if the sellers would be open to something creative."

Again, I leave it at that and say nothing more. Sometimes they will volunteer a long explanation of what the seller will or will not do or sometimes they say, "Like what?"

"Well, something like a rent-to-own or a lease option. I am a rent-to-own buyer looking for a home in this area. Would your seller be open to something like that?"

Don't say anything until they respond. You'll get one of five responses:

> *"Yes, they have mentioned that to me." If you*
> *get a positive response, the next question to*
> *ask is, "Great, do you know what kind of*
> *terms they are looking for or are they looking*
> *for an offer?"*

If they are looking for terms that work for you or they are looking for an offer, make an appointment with Sally agent to look at the home. Note: Sally will try to become your Realtor®. This might not be bad if Sally is creative and willing to read this book along with you, but otherwise don't sign anything to commit you to Sally except for this home. If Sally is really good, you might want her to be your agent. If the terms are not within your scope, then ask the following:

> *"Do you have any other listings where your*
> *seller might have said to you, 'Sally*
> *(remember to use their real name☺), if you*
> *don't sell my home soon I might have to rent*
> *it?' Sally, can you think of any of your*
> *listings like this that might work for me?"*

> *Use this follow-up sentence on any of the*
> *statements below where it applies. You*
> *always want to dig to see what else they have*
> *that might work for you.*

Sally may also respond to the rent-to-own question like this:

> *"No, they need to sell now and wouldn't be*
> *interested in that."*

If this is the case, jump right to the question where you ask if she has any other listings that might work. You will need to know your price range and what you can afford; as she will probably ask you about this (we covered this in Chapter 3).

> *"I'm not sure; I would have to check with*
> *them."*

If this is the response, encourage the agent to talk with her clients. Remind her that you are looking for a rent-to-own home in that area and her commission would be paid in full when you buy the home.

"What are you talking about?"

Not every agent knows what rent-to-own is so you may need to give them a brief explanation. Be prepared to tell them something like, *"Well I would rent the home and buy it later."* Keep it simple.

"Why do you need a rent-to-own?"

Most likely it's because you can't get a mortgage right now or because you don't want to get a mortgage right now. Your best answer is to simply tell her that a mortgage won't work for you now, but you do want to get into a home now and ask her if this home or another listing of hers might be a candidate for rent-to-own. Keep your answer brief, but do be honest. If you had a bankruptcy or a foreclosure, it will be important that they know that. Don't spring that on them later. If you had perfect credit, you probably wouldn't need a rent-to-own in the first place.

The "For Rent" Ads

When it comes to finding sellers in the newspaper or on-line sites such as <u>Craigslist.org</u>, I prefer to look for homes listed "For Rent" versus "For Sale". This may sound funny when you are looking to buy a home, not just rent it, but it works. The reason for this is that many sellers who don't or can't sell their home decide they should rent it. This is the type of seller we are looking for when we call the "For Rent" ads. Their motivation is higher than most sellers and this is what we want.

Many of the sellers in the "For Sale" section MUST sell their home outright and don't have the flexibility to do a rent-to-own. They can't get another mortgage or move on with their life until that home is sold, so a rent-to-own just won't work for them. Many of the homes listed for rent, especially in down real estate markets, are actually homes that sellers are trying to sell, but have not been able to. This means they've put it up for rent because they are tired of paying a mortgage on an empty home that hasn't sold. These sellers have already accepted the idea of having renters in their home PLUS they still want to sell. This is the perfect seller for you!

I have found that even in stronger real estate markets, 30% to 50% of people I call in the "For Rent" ads will consider a rent-to-own if you know how to ask them. In soft real estate markets, the percentage will be higher. Also, a big part of talking with these sellers is building rapport – be friendly on the phone. You are going to be asking someone to offer you his or her home for little or no money down and the right to buy it. People will do more for you when they like you, and they will like you more when you are friendly.

Script to Use When Calling "For Rent" Ads

You'll have the best success if you use this script:

> *"Hi, my name is _____ and I was calling about your home for rent." Giving your name sounds warmer and will help put the owner at ease with you.*

> *"Can you tell me if it is still available?"*

> *If yes, continue. "When is it available?" If not, say "Okay thanks for your time" and hang up.*

> *"Can you tell me a little about the home?"*

Let them give some information about the home. Or expand with some questions from the ad. Remember, you are building rapport with the owner. Talk and let them talk. People warm up when they are the ones talking. Listen, and sound interested in what they are saying. This is also how you'll determine whether this home will meet your needs.

> *"When was the home built?"*

This question gives you insight into any updating you might run into. If the home is older, ask the next question, if it is newer you will skip this question.

> *"Have the kitchen and bathroom(s) been*
> *updated since it was built?"*

If it was built in the 70's, I might ask if the baths or kitchens are yellow/green/brown or if they have been updated since it was built. I am primarily building rapport and leading up to the main question.

> *"Does it have a garage or basement?"*

Of course, don't ask if it has a basement if you are in Florida or any other location where they wouldn't have basements. Ask what is relevant to your area. Don't ask questions that are answered in the ad or what they have already told you. Ask questions applicable to your area of the country (Is it in a flood area? Does it have central air? Has it ever had termites? Whatever might be of interest to you and to find out more about the home).

> *"Is the yard fenced?"*

This may prompt them to ask the question as to whether or not you have pets. Of course, be honest. If you have a dog and they don't want dogs, you might be out of luck; however, if you can meet them, you might be able to build enough rapport that they won't care if you have pets. If they like you, they'll be more likely to want to sell/rent to you.

They may also ask questions as to how many people will be living in the home or how many kids you have. The second part is not legal; it's a violation of Fair Housing Law, which I'll talk about in Chapter 15. Unfortunately, many people do not know this. Don't take offense to it; your goal is to buy a home. If they refuse you because you have kids, refer to Chapter 15 regarding how to handle it.

If the home sounds like something you would like to own or at least want to see, then pop the question:

> *"Wow, this home sounds really nice, would
> you considering selling it?"*

If they say *"No"* then say,

> *"Well, thanks for your time, but I am really
> looking for something I can rent-to-own,
> something like a lease with an option to buy.
> Are you sure you won't consider something
> like this?"*

Leave them your name and number to contact you later if they change their mind about selling. If this is a home you think you would really like, follow up in a month (if you can wait that long), ask if it is still available and see if they might have changed their mind. Sometimes an owner might not want to sell when you call, but their motivation may have changed or increased by the time you follow up.

If they say "M*aybe*" or "Y*es*", ask if you can see their home. What we are really looking for is the seller who couldn't sell his home on his own or with a real estate agent, so he decided to rent it. When you ask the question and he says, *"Yes, I will sell it! It's listed now but it hasn't sold, so that is why we decided to rent it."* Bingo! You've found a potential rent-to-own. Now you just need to see the home and use the information in this book to make an offer, if you decide you want to buy it.

You might, however, follow up with some of these questions:

> *"Can you tell me how much you would want
> for the home?"*

Make sure that it is within your price range. Start to feel out the owner for the type of terms they would consider.

> *"When are you available for me to see the
> home to see if I would be interested in it?"*

Then set it up! Keep building rapport with the seller.

Distressed Builders

Have you dreamed of owning a brand new home? A home that no one has lived in before? You might think that because you can't qualify for a mortgage right now it isn't possible to buy a brand new home.

The fact is that many home builders are hurting in soft markets. In some areas, sales of new construction are down as much or <u>more</u> than existing homes. When builders are hurting, they may have to get creative. Not all builders can do rent-to-owns, but there certainly are some who can. In fact, a few builders are even advertising their homes as rent-to-owns!

Obviously, if you are looking for a brand new home, a builder who is advertising homes as rent-to-own is a great place to start. If you can't find a rent-to-own or their homes don't suit your price or needs, try other builders.

Many builders right now are offering their homes for rent and for sale simultaneously. If you see a "For Rent" sign on a new construction home, you can pretty much be certain that the builder doesn't just want to rent it, they want to sell it. Since they already have accepted the possibility of renters, the battle is half over in getting them to agree to a rent-to-own.

A builder who is offering a home just "For Sale" and not "For Rent" is still a possibility, but be prepared for more rejections with these builders.

Most, if not all, new construction homes are listed in the MLS. That means if you are working with a real estate agent, he or she can search for new construction homes that fit your needs. However, before you look at them, your agent should check to see if the builder is willing to consider something like rent-to-own.

I would recommend that your agent first start searching for new construction rental listings (and of course, new construction rent-to-own listings). Your agent will need to contact the listing agent and follow the script in Chapter 21.

If you aren't working with a real estate agent, you'll need to find builders on your own. You can do this much the way you would if you were contacting listing agents. Begin by driving around areas you would like to live and make note of the contact information for new construction homes. Larger developments will have a sales office on site, while smaller ones will have "For Sale" signs in front of the homes for sale. Stop by the sales trailer and talk to the sales person or call them and use the following script:

Script for Buyer When Calling a Listing Agent About a

New Construction House

Call the contact person from the sign or advertisement and say:

> *"Hi Sally, my name is _____ and I was calling about the home you have listed at _____ (the address). Is it still available?"*

> *After they say, "Yes, it is," I would say:*

"Can you tell me more about the home? How much is it and how large is it?"

Listen to see if it is something you would be interested in. If so, follow up with:

"I wondered if the builder would be open to something creative."

Leave it at that and say nothing more. Your goal is for them to launch into a long explanation of what the seller will or will not do. Other times they'll say, *"Like what?"*

"Well, something like a rent-to-own or a lease option. I am a rent-to-own buyer looking for a new home in this area. Would the builder be open to something like this?"

Like before, you will probably get several possible responses:

1. "Yes, they have mentioned that to me." If you get a positive response, then ask: "Great! Do you know what kind of terms they are looking for or are they looking for an offer?"

If they are looking for terms that work for you or they are looking for an offer, make an appointment to see the home if you haven't already. If you are working with a real estate agent, you should tell the salesperson on-site that you have an agent and tell her who it is. Call your agent to tell him you found something you are interested in. Even though the sales person on-site can show you the home and amenities, your agent can still help you with the transaction.

If the terms are not within your budget, ask the following:

"Do you have any other new construction listings where your builder might have said to

you, 'Sally, if you don't sell that home soon, I might have to rent it,' Sally, can you think of any of your listings that might work for me?"

Sally may also respond to the rent-to-own question like this:

2. "No, they need to sell now and wouldn't be interested in that."

If this is the case, jump right to the question where you ask if she has any other listings that might work. You will need to know your price range and what you can afford; as she will probably ask you about this (we covered this in Chapter 3).

3. "I'm not sure. I would have to check with them."

If this is the response, encourage the agent to talk with her builder and to call you as soon as she knows.

4. "What are you talking about?"

If she doesn't know what rent-to-own is, you may have to give her a brief explanation.

5. "Why do you need a rent-to-own?"

Your best answer is to simply tell her that a mortgage won't work for you now, but you do want to get into a home now. Ask her if this home or another listing of hers might be a candidate for rent-to-own. Keep your answer brief and let her ask you more questions if she has them.

For Sale by Owners

The last method I use to find motivated sellers are "FSBO's", or "For Sale by Owners". I use this one the least because so many of these owners need to sell their home now. They can't do a rent-to-own because it would prevent them from getting into another home themselves.

That being said, however, there are definitely FSBO's out there that can do rent-to-owns. It may just take more phone calls than the other techniques. If you are working with a real estate agent, you may have to pay their commission yourself as many FSBO's don't offer commission to agents. You can find FSBO's either in the newspaper ads, the Internet or by driving around neighborhoods you are interested in.

Script for Buyers to Call FSBO's
(For Sale by Owner Homes)

Once you have a list of sellers you want to call, use this script. It is very similar to the For Rent script with a few key changes:

"Hi, my name is _____ and I was calling about your home for sale. Can you tell me if it is still available?"

If yes, continue.

"Can you tell me a little about the home?"

Let them give you some information about the home. You are building rapport with the owner. Talk and let them talk. People warm up when they are the ones talking. Listen and sound interested. This is also how you'll determine whether this home will meet your needs.

"When was the home built?"

This question gives you insight into any updating you might run into. If the home is older, ask the next question, if it is newer you will skip this question.

> *"Have the kitchen and bathroom(s) been*
> *updated since it was built?"*

If it was built in the 1970's, I might ask if the baths or kitchens are yellow/green/brown or if they have been updated since it was built. I am primarily building rapport and leading up to the main question.

> *"Does it have a garage or basement?"*

Don't ask questions that are answered in the ad or what they have already told you. Ask questions applicable to your area of the country (Is it in a flood area? Does it have central air? Has it ever had termites? Whatever might be of interest to you and to find out more about the home).

> *"Is the yard fenced?"*

If the home sounds like something you would like to own or at least want to see, pop the following question:

> *"Your home sounds really great and it might*
> *be just what I'm looking for. Do you think you*
> *would consider something creative like rent-*
> *to-own or a lease option sale?"*
>
> *Wait for a response. As in other cases, you*
> *are going to get one of four answers.*
>
> *1. "Yes, I've thought about renting it, so rent-*
> *to-own might work."*
>
> *If you get a positive response, ask:*
>
> *"Great, do you know what kind of terms you*
> *are looking for or are you looking for an*
> *offer?"*

If they are looking for terms that work for you or they are looking for an offer, make an appointment to look at the home. If the terms are outside of your range, thank them and move on.

2. "No, I need to sell it now and wouldn't be interested in that."

If they say no, thank them for their time and move on to the next one.

3. "I'm not sure. I would have to think about it."

In this case, you may want to make an appointment to look at the house so that you and the seller can talk more about rent-to-own in person. You'll build more rapport with the seller if you meet in person and they'll be more likely to consider it.

4. "What are you talking about?"

It's entirely possible that the seller has no idea what rent-to-own is, so you may need to explain it.

Now that you've seen ways to go out and find rent-to-own homes, how about some methods to get sellers to come to you? That's right; instead of you tracking down properties and calling sellers, they'll call you instead and offer you their home as a rent-to-own. In the next chapter, we'll look at exactly that – getting sellers to call you.

Chapter 6:

How to Get Sellers to Call You

Now that you've learned ways to find rent-to-own homes, what would you say to having rent-to-own *sellers call you and offer you their home*? That's right. You can just sit by the phone and wait for sellers to call you and tell you about their rent-to-own home.

Many of these sellers will not have their homes listed with a real estate agent, so if you are working with an agent, this chapter may not be for you. While you can certainly follow the techniques in this chapter, if you are working with an agent, you may have to pay your agent's commission if the seller won't.

This also involves a little more work on your part, whereas if you are working with a Realtor®, she will likely be putting in most of the effort toward finding you a rent-to-own home. While it will involve more work for you than if your Realtor® finds you the home, it may involve less work than you trying to find rent-to-own sellers on your own, as in the previous chapter.

The advantage of having the seller call you is that you already know he is willing to consider rent-to-own. You just need to figure out if his home and terms will work for you.

"Alright Wendy! So how do I do this?"

There are a couple of ways to get sellers to come to you.

Posting Ads

The first way is by posting ads about yourself and rent-to-own. Here are two examples:

Can't sell your home? Thought about renting it?

I'm looking to rent with an option to buy.

We could be the perfect match!

(123) 456-7890

Tired of your home sitting for sale?

Is it empty and the payment is

harder to make each month?

Buyer wants to lease option your home!

Call today

(123) 456-7890

These are sample ads of what you would put in the newspaper where space is an issue – the more space you use the more it costs you. These ads though are just enough to get the attention of a home seller who has started to think about what choices he must make if he doesn't sell soon.

You can also post a longer ad on FREE sites like Craigslist, Yahoo! groups and Google groups. I also recommend posting some flyers on community bulletin boards as well as posting flyers using these FREE Internet sites. These methods are much cheaper than the newspaper classified ads and may be all you need.

With a longer ad, you might want to go with something like this:

Can't sell your home? Thought about renting it?

I am a buyer looking to rent and then buy. As a future home buyer, I don't have the tenant mentality that scares most sellers from renting their homes.

I want to buy a home, but can't get a mortgage quite yet.

Renting-to-buy is the perfect solution for both of us. You can stop worrying about that mortgage payment and I can find my new home now!

Call me to find out how this could work for both of us.

(123) 456-7890

The whole purpose of these ads is to filter out the home sellers who don't want tenants and to get the ones that would consider tenants to call you. Once they call you, use this script (you'll see it is very similar to the ones in Chapter 5):

Call Home Sellers' Advertisements

Script to use when Seller calls about your ad:

Seller calls and says:

"Hello, I was calling about your ad in Craigslist."

"Great! My name is Joe, what is your name?" It's always good to use names; it sounds warmer and helps to start building rapport. In this case, we'll say the seller's name is Jane.

"Jane, where is your home located?" Is it an area you are interested in?

"Can you tell me what price you are looking to get for your home?" Is it in your price range? If not, don't waste your time or theirs.

"Jane, can you tell me a little bit about your home? How many bedrooms and baths does it have?" You should probably take some notes to record the details.

"What is the approximate square footage?"

"Jane, do you know when the home was built?"

This question gives you insight into any updating you might run into. If the home is older, ask the next question, if it is newer you will skip this question.

"Have the kitchen and bathroom(s) been updated since it was built?"

If it was built in the 1970's, I might ask if the baths or kitchens are yellow/green/brown or if they have been updated since it was built.

"Does it have a garage or basement?"

Of course, don't ask if it has a basement if you are in Florida or another location where they wouldn't have basements. Ask what is relevant to your area (Is it in a flood area? Does it have central air? Has it ever had termites? Ask whatever might be of interest to you to find out more about the home).

"Is the yard fenced?"

This may prompt them to ask the question about whether or not you have pets. Of course, be honest. If you have a dog and they don't want dogs, you might be out of luck; however, if you can meet them, you might also be able to build enough rapport that they won't care if you have pets. If they like you, they'll be more likely to want to sell/rent to you.

They may also ask questions as to how many people will be living in the home or how many kids you have. The second part is not legal; it's a violation of Fair Housing Law, which I'll talk about in Chapter 15. Unfortunately, many people do not know this. Don't take offense to it. Your goal is to buy a home. If they refuse you because you have kids, refer to Chapter 15 regarding how to handle this situation.

"Jane, your home sounds pretty nice so far. What other features does the home have that you think I should know about?"

Because you don't have a seller's ad to start from, you'll need to get a little more information about the home directly from the seller. Does the home meet your basic needs? If you need a four-bedroom home and Jane's home has only two, it's not a match for you. But if Jane's home is close to what you need, you'll want to continue to get more information.

"Jane, do you know what the rental rates are in your area? About how much were you thinking for monthly rent?"

Notice how I asked first about area rental rates? Many home sellers think that the monthly rental rate should be equal to or greater than their mortgage payment, even if the mortgage payment is more than the going rental rate. If you are interested in making an offer on the home later, you'll need to do some checking to find out what the comparable prices are and what the market rents are. You can't just take the seller's word for it because usually they either don't know or they are asking too much.

If the asking price and rent are within your budget or at least somewhat close to your budget (you can always try to negotiate them down), you should make an appointment to look at the home. Don't get into too many details about the option fee, option credits, length of the lease and so forth over the phone. Wait until you meet with her and are ready to make an offer. This way you will have built up much more rapport with her and she will be more interested in selling you her home as a rent-to-own.

Before you make the appointment, the seller is probably going to want to know a little bit about rent-to-own, too.

> *"Jane, your home sounds very interesting to me. What I am looking for is a home that I can rent with an option to buy. In other words, I would rent it from you for a period of time, and at the end of the rental period I can buy it from you. This gives me time to improve my credit and qualify for a mortgage. I would like to make an appointment with you to look at your home and we can talk more about this."*

Real Estate Investors

Another great way to get sellers to contact you is to go to local real estate investment group meetings. Real estate investors are always looking for buyers. To find an investor group near you, I recommend searching Google for either your city name or your county name and "real estate investor group" or association. For example, "Oakland County Real Estate Investor Association" or "Atlanta Real Estate Investor Group".

There are two types of investors at these meetings who will want to work with you; the *rehabbers* and the *sandwich lease option* investors. The rehabbers are investors who have bought a home that needs fixing up, repaired it and are now reselling it. Rehabbers prefer to find conventional buyers just like other home sellers, but given the state of most real estate markets, they recognize the need to be flexible and many will consider a rent-to-own A sandwich lease option investor makes their money by creating a spread between the deal they work out with the seller and the deal they work out with the buyer. They are doing two rent-to-owns with one home; one from the seller and one to the buyer.

The advantage of working with rehabbers is that you get a newly renovated home, which means it may have some of the following: a new roof, new kitchen, new bath, new flooring, fresh paint, etc. Freshly rehabbed homes can often be the best home on the market in a particular neighborhood. The disadvantage many rehabbers have is that the home they are selling is usually completely empty. Most buyers have trouble visualizing living in an empty home. That can make it difficult to sell.

To find investors, I recommend going to one or several of the investor group meetings. Once there, you have two choices. The first is a little bold, but can have great results, and that is to introduce yourself in front of the group. Tell them that you are interested in buying a rent-to-own home, what you are looking for (i.e. how many bedrooms, baths, special needs, etc.) and what your price range is. Then let them come to you.

Your second choice is to network more quietly. Talk with a few people. Tell them who you are and ask if they know of lease option or rehab investors you could talk to.

Either way, you are likely to find people who are interested in working with you. This is what investors do. Talk with them about their home, much like in the script above to find out details about the property. If they have something that fits your needs, make an appointment to look at the home.

In the next chapter, we will start looking at the paperwork. I know…everyone's favorite topic. Trust me though; it really doesn't have to be that bad, especially if you are using my course - I will walk you through it step-by-step. The paperwork is also very important to you because it can make a huge difference in the deal you get, both in terms of protecting you legally and also giving you better financial terms.

PART 3:

UNDERSTANDING THE PAPERWORK

Chapter 7

Rental Agreements

Okay, here comes the fun part: the paperwork! No seriously, it is not that complex or scary, but it can seem overwhelming if you don't take it one piece at a time. This process of rent-to-own can seem a bit complex, so I'll try to keep it simple.

There are many ideas and suggestions in this book for those who want every detail. Some do, some don't. Some will go through it all, some won't. It is here so you can use what works for you, and what you feel comfortable with. In this chapter, I refer to you, the buyer, as the *tenant* and the seller is the *owner,* or *landlord.* Let's dig right in.

The Basics

The *Rental Agreement* (a.k.a. *Lease Agreement*) is basically an agreement between you and the landlord that defines the terms of the rental period. These are the basic points it covers:

- How long you can rent the home (in a rent-to-own, you can purchase it before the end of the rental period – unless it states otherwise)
- What you will pay each month for your rental payment
- Where and how you will pay the landlord
- The amount of the Security deposit and where the landlord will hold your deposit
- Any other provisions, such as late fees, bounced check fees, rental agreement violations, etc.
- And, of course, the required lead based paint language which alerts you to a potential hazard

Fill in the Blanks

It isn't necessary to go over a rental agreement in detail because you don't need to know every detail to rent-to-own your new home.

Most good Rental Agreements take the guesswork out of the picture for you, making your life significantly easier. They do this by having all of the regular terms and conditions pre-printed. When it comes to completing the details that are specific to YOUR rent-to-own purchase, you simply fill in the blanks. You will fill in how long the rental agreement lasts, how much the monthly rent will be, the security deposit, and so forth.

Wendy's Wisdom

You should never draft your own rental agreements (or any other contracts for that matter) from scratch. Always use pre-created contracts (preferably pro-buyer) and just fill in the relevant details. Creating your own contracts can cause you enormous headaches and potential legal problems.

Pro-Buyer vs. Neutral

Not all paperwork and contracts are created equally. In fact, there are three different types of contracts: *Pro-Seller, Neutral* and *Pro-Buyer*. I have contracts that protect me when I am selling, but I have different ones to protect me when I am buying. I call these my "pro-seller" and "pro-buyer" contracts. You, as the buyer, will want pro-buyer contracts for your transaction, whenever possible. You can order these on my website if you don't already have them. They offer you the most protection and the most favorable terms.

You usually do NOT want to accept the rental agreement from a seller or the seller's agent, if you can avoid it. He will be, AT BEST, neutral. Try to have your buyer's agent provide the seller/listing agent with a copy of your rental agreement when you make your offer. This way he can include your pro-buyer rental agreement. If the seller has an issue with any of the terms in your rental agreement, you can always negotiate. If the seller won't accept your rental agreement, I suggest you use my pro-buyer clauses and try to add those to their contract.

Wendy's Wisdom

Not all contracts are the same. Protect yourself by making sure you have "pro-buyer" contracts – even if you are working with a real estate agent.

You might not want to use the rental agreement your real estate agent has (unless he has mine or they are pro-buyer), as he typically has only one set of contracts and they are usually neutral. If you choose to work with a real estate agent when buying your home on a rent-to-own basis, you can still use the contracts you get from my course, as they will be much more favorable to you (or update the agent's contracts with my clauses to protect you). It is an easy change for your real estate agent to add a few favorable clauses for you.

How Much of a Difference Can it Make for You?

Here is just one example. If you use the lease from a real estate agent or from the seller, you might end up being responsible for ALL repairs to the property during your rental period. If the furnace quits, one of the appliances breaks down, the plumbing springs a leak or worse during the rental, you could be stuck paying! That could cost you thousands of extra dollars. If you use the pro-buyer contracts, the seller is responsible for all repairs, or you can choose to share the expenses. Sharing the expenses can be done any way you can work out with the seller. For instance, you might pay the first $500 and he pays anything above that, or you split all repairs 60/40, they pay 60%. Any way you do this; if he pays part or all of the repairs, it will mean big savings to you. You need the savings during your option period so that you can pay off debt and save for your home.

Key Clauses

Here are several of the clauses you will find in my rental agreements that make them pro-buyer.

Insurance

Owner agrees to continue to carry homeowner's insurance on this home and to have the policy changed to a non-owner occupied insurance policy.

It's very important that the owner continue insurance. He is responsible for insuring his home during the rental period, not you.

This is important for a couple of reasons. First, should any covered damage happen to the home, the insurance policy will handle any repairs. Second, if the seller has a mortgage on the home, he could be violating the terms of the mortgage if he fails to keep the property insured.

You will want to obtain renter's insurance to protect your possessions, but the home itself must be insured by the owner (seller). Once you own the home, you will be required to change your policy to a homeowner's policy.

Maintenance, Repairs or Alterations

The Landlord gives the tenant the right to make repairs or improvements to the property at the tenant's expense.

All repairs will be done by the tenant's contractors unless otherwise specified.

This is where you will want to put in who will pay for what repairs. This clause states that you can choose to make repairs to the home, but you will want to decide who pays for the changes and adjust this wording, if the owner is paying a portion or all of the repairs. I personally like the owner to pay for repairs during the option period when I am the buyer.

Wendy's Wisdom

Be careful not to put too much into a home you don't own. If everything doesn't work out, then you would lose those repairs. Do them in moderation; I do not recommend finishing an entire home.

Rental Payments

It is very important when you are doing a lease option that you make SURE the seller is paying his mortgage payment. If he doesn't pay it, your dream will become a nightmare. I recommend you have your monthly payment made *to their mortgage company* versus to the seller directly. It is very important that you put the loan number in the memo and with the letter, if you are mailing it to the lender. You can also set up an automatic payment plan to come directly from your checking account. The main thing to agree on is what your rental payment will be. If your payment is $1,500 to the seller and the mortgage payment is $1,600, he will need to pay $100 toward his mortgage each month. If his mortgage payment is $1,200, you can pay him $300 and the mortgage company $1,200; but either way, this must get paid each month or you will be without a house.

You will want to put the mortgage information in the rental agreement where it states who you pay and where it will be mailed, if this is what you agree to. You can also agree to send it to a third party, such as an escrow company. They will handle the payment and notify either side if something is wrong.

Majestic Realty	*www.WendyPatton.com*	289765
4742 W. Clarkston Road	Date_____	
Clarkston, MI 48348		

Pay to the order of ____ **BANK ONE** _____ | **$1,100**

Eleven hundred and 00/100--Dollars

memo *Loan #123456*   *Wendy Patton*

Late Fees

As far as late fees are concerned, keep those to a minimum or zero, just in case you have a month where you are a few days late. Note that being late can cause a problem for you when you apply for a mortgage in the future, but a few days should not affect it.

Your rental agreement should be short and simple. Most rental agreements will have many more clauses, but they are usually not good for you. This is why removing them and redrafting a new agreement with fewer clauses (or using my agreements) is a good idea. A few things that might be in a rental agreement that are okay are the security deposit section and the Lead-Based Paint Disclosure. There might also be other state required clauses (California is known for these). The Lead-Based Paint Disclosure is federal law, but the security deposit will be dictated by state or local law. If you can put your "down payment/option fee" into the security deposit versus in the Option Agreement, it will become refundable for you if you choose not to or can't purchase the home.

In the next chapter, we will cover the Option Agreement.

Chapter 8

Option Agreements

The *Option Agreement* gives you, the tenant-buyer, the right to buy the seller's home at a later date. It is binding only to the seller, meaning that the option agreement prevents the seller from selling the home to anyone else as long as the option is valid, but you are not obligated to buy the home. The option agreement does, however, set some terms and conditions which could invalidate your option to buy the home and release the seller, allowing them to sell their home to someone else.

The Basics

The Option Agreement is really fairly short and simple. These are the basic points it covers:

- The amount of the option fee, if any

- When and how it will be paid

- The date range during which the option is valid

- Whether there will be any additional option credits applied from your rental payment – **this is KEY**

- A statement that indicates your option fee is non-refundable if you choose not to purchase the home

What the Option Agreement Does Not Contain

Almost as important as what it *does* contain is what it *does not*. The option agreement usually does not contain any details about the purchase price. Those details are contained in the Sales Contract. It does not contain any details about financing. It also doesn't contain details about the Rental Agreement. Each of these contracts is separate for a reason.

Wendy's Wisdom

In general, clearing up credit always takes longer than expected, so if you think it will take a year to do so, add on an additional six months to the contract. Always give yourself an additional 6-12 months at minimum. The date of final sale should reflect this.

Fill in the Blanks

Like the Rental Agreement, the Option Agreement should have all of the standard information pre-printed. This leaves you with the responsibility of filling in the blanks that are specifically pertinent to the purchase of your home. You would fill in such blanks as who the *optionee* (you) and who the *optionor* (seller) are. Other key points you would fill in would be the amount of the option fee and the date range the option is valid. Don't try to draft up an entire option agreement or any other paperwork on your own. I guarantee you will miss many of the essential details.

Pro-Buyer vs. Neutral

Like the Rental Agreement, Option Agreements can be pro-seller, neutral or pro-buyer. Believe me, it does make a difference!

Your best bet would be to use the contracts / agreements from my website. I have been using them and improving on them for more than twenty years. If you elect not to purchase them, I would recommend you retain the services of an attorney to help you get the most protection possible. Explore Pre-Paid Legal services at www.GotLegalPlans.com to get the best rates and advice.

Wendy's Wisdom

I cannot stress how important it is to seek help. Use pro-buyer contracts to help you with your paperwork. Use a real estate agent or an attorney to assist you with the purchase of your home. It will make your life so much easier.

Key Clauses

Here are several of the clauses you will find in my Option Agreement that make it pro-buyer. Remember, you are the *optionee* and the seller is the *optionor*.

Exclusive Right

> *Optionor grants Optionee the exclusive right to exercise this option for a period commencing on _____, and terminating at midnight, _____. If not exercised, this option shall expire at midnight _____ and Optionor shall be released from all obligations hereunder, legal or equitable.*

This clause protects you by giving you the exclusive right to buy during the option period. The seller cannot sell their home to anyone else as long as the option is valid. Note that once the option expires, the seller is allowed to keep the option fee if you don't buy the home.

Option Credits

> *There shall be additional option consideration of $_____ per month given by Optionor to Optionee as credit towards purchasing this home. This monthly option consideration shall be credited toward the down payment/purchase price of the above property.*

This clause is critical and can be worth many thousands of dollars to you. It is another important reason to have pro-buyer contracts, as neutral and pro-seller contracts will almost certainly not have this clause.

Option Credits are amounts that are credited against the purchase price when you buy the home. Typically, they are applied out of the monthly rent. For example, if you are paying $1,000 per month in rent, you might ask for $750 in option credits. The initial amount you ask for will be negotiable with the seller. If $750 seems like a lot to you, remember the seller can negotiate it down, but they certainly won't negotiate it up. It's not a bad idea to ask for more than you want initially so that you can settle on a number close to what you actually want. At the same time, if $750 seems small, you could even ask for the full $1,000 to be applied as option credits. Yes, I <u>have</u> received the full rent amount applied as option credits!

Whatever amount you agree upon, for example $500 per month, will accumulate each month of the option period. If the option period is 24 months, you would accumulate $12,000 towards the purchase price. That makes for a pretty nice down payment especially when it's coming out of what you would normally pay in rent.

Option credits, like the option fee, only apply against the purchase price of the home, so if you don't buy the home, you won't receive these credits.

No Liens

> *Optionor agrees they will not put any additional liens against property before or during option period. Additional liens would also imply unpaid property taxes, IRS liens, second mortgages, etc.*

Additional liens against the home may impact your ability to purchase the home. For example, if the seller fails to pay their property taxes, it would create a lien against the property preventing the seller from selling the home until the taxes are paid. Typically, the taxes would be paid out of proceeds at the closing, but if the seller doesn't have enough equity, the taxes cannot be paid, and you will not be able to buy the home. This is why you want to buy from sellers with some equity in their home and not over-leveraged. If they don't have any equity and they didn't pay their tax bill, they would have to come up with this amount to sell their home to you. What if they don't have these funds and you are ready to buy the home? Do you think they will be able to give you back the money you have invested? No. Make sure the seller is in good shape with some equity (more to come on this later).

Direct Payment

> *If Optionor doesn't pay their mortgage payment, property insurance or tax payments, then the Optionee has the right to pay the rental amount directly to either of these parties, versus the seller. If any amount paid to either of these parties exceeds the amount due that month, then the additional amount paid by Optionee will be credited at closing to the Optionee – with an additional 50% added as credit. (i.e. if the rental amount is $900 and the payment made for*

> *mortgage or taxes is $1000 – then the purchaser*
> *would be credited at closing $100 + $50 = $150*
> *off the purchase price).*

This clause is all about protecting <u>you</u> to ensure that you will be able to purchase the home, even if the seller stops making payments. It gives you the right to make the payment directly if the seller stops paying his mortgage. Obviously, we don't want the seller to stop making his payments, but if for some reason that does happen, you can take over payments and insure that you are able to buy the home later.

Additionally, should this happen and you end up having to pay more than your monthly rental amount to keep the payments current, not only would that extra amount be credited against the purchase price, but you would also receive half again as much as a credit (as in the example).

Wendy's Wisdom

Do the contracts seem intimidating to you? Remember, your real estate agent and your Pre-Paid Legal attorney can help you. This takes most of the burden off your shoulders.

That covers the Option Agreement. In the next chapter, we will look at the Sales Contract, which defines the terms and conditions for you to purchase the seller's home.

Chapter 9

Sales Contract

The *Sales Contract* is sometimes called *Offer to Purchase, Purchase Contract, Purchase Sales Contract, Sales Agreement* or a multitude of similar names. The most common is the *Sales Contract*. This contract outlines and details the terms and conditions of the purchase of your home. In this chapter, you will be called the *purchaser* and the seller will be the *seller*.

For the most part, if you are working with a real estate agent, you will be using his contract. Most states require real estate agents to use their state approved sales contract. You can still add some clauses to an existing contract.

The Basics

These are the basic points the Sales Contract covers:

- The agreed upon purchase price

- Any personal property that will come with the sale of the home (appliances, pool tables, hot tubs or anything not attached to the home)

- If there will be an inspection of the home (highly recommended) and what the conditions of the inspection will be

- What type of financing you will use to purchase the home (In the case of an option, it will not be contingent upon financing. You will have your option time period to get ready for a mortgage, but if you are not approved, you will lose your option fee and the right to buy the home)

- What type of title insurance will be provided and who will pay

- In some states, there are very specific clauses that must be included in your sales contract (California has many)

- If there is a real estate broker involved, there will be clauses about their role and exclusion from liability for the entire transaction

What the Sales Contract Does Not Contain

The Sales Contract usually does not contain anything about what amount was put down as an option fee. This is only in the Option Agreement. It doesn't mention the dates of when the offer (Sales Contract) is valid. It only refers to "See attached Option Agreement signed this same day."

Fill in the Blanks

Much of the Sales Contract is standard, but you will need to fill in some information. You will need the purchase price, the property's legal description and the physical address. This is the main part of what you fill in.

Pro-Buyer

Like the other agreements, sales contracts can be pro-seller, neutral or pro-buyer. It makes a difference.

Key Clauses

Here are several of the clauses you will find in my Sales Agreement that make it pro-buyer.

Default

> *In the event of default by Purchaser, Seller may, at his option, declare forfeiture hereunder and retain the option deposit (if any) as full and complete liquidated damages. In the event of default by Seller, the seller must pay damages to the purchaser in the amount equal to all option monies applied, any improvements made to the home or property, and all attorney fees to the purchaser within 30 days of notice from purchaser OR purchaser may, at his option, elect to enforce the terms hereof. Seller also agrees to pay for any attorney fees associated with a default.*

You would definitely not find this clause in a neutral or pro-seller contract. If you default as the purchaser, the seller's sole remedy is whatever option fee you've already paid. This doesn't give you the right to trash the home or steal things; they can pursue you for damages under the rental agreement. It simply means that if you don't purchase the home, you are only out the option fee.

If the seller defaults they owe you the option fee, plus the value of any improvements you made to the property (not just your cost for material, but the actual value of the improvement), plus attorney's fees.

Title Objections

> *If Purchaser objects to title he must notify Seller of the same within ten days of receipt of evidence of title. Seller must rectify all title problems within 30 days of such notice, or must pay the Purchaser the amount equal to all option monies applied to purchase, plus any improvements that Purchaser has made to the property, plus any attorney fees associated with title problems, all within 30 days of notice from Purchaser of this contract. If both*

> *Seller and Purchaser agree to extend the contract to solve title problems beyond the option period, it must be in writing and signed by both parties.*

The seller must provide you with a clear title when you buy the home. If they don't or can't, this clause defines what happens. The penalties for title objections are much the same as those for default. If you have accumulated any option credits, the seller would have to pay you for those as well.

Property Inspection

> *The Purchaser(s) may have the physical condition, structural, plumbing, heating, and electrical systems of the property inspected by a contractor of his own choice within ____ # of days, ____ days from the date of acceptance of this offer and at his own expense. If seller does not receive written notice from the purchaser(s) of their dissatisfaction regarding said inspection within 2 days from date of inspection, then this contingency will be considered satisfied and the purchase agreement is binding without regard to said report. If the seller does receive written notice, within the time provided, that purchaser(s) are dissatisfied, purchaser(s) at their election may terminate this agreement and all deposited monies shall be returned to purchaser(s).*

I cannot emphasize this enough – GET AN INSPECTION! There is a chapter later in the book on inspections, so I won't go into details here. To put it simply, however, you want an inspection to help identify potential problems. This is protection for you and it is well worth the cost.

If the inspection is unsatisfactory and there are just too many problems with the house, you can terminate the sales contract and all deposit money will be returned to you.

Non-Payment

> *If Seller doesn't pay their mortgage payment, property insurance or tax payments, then the Purchaser has the right to pay the rental amount directly to either of these parties, versus the seller. If any amount paid to either of these parties exceeds the amount due that month, then the additional amount paid by Purchaser will be credited at closing to the Purchaser – with an additional 50% added as credit.*

This is the same as in the Option Agreement, however, if you are paying the mortgage directly as we discussed in the Rental Agreement chapter, then this is only necessary to cover taxes, insurance, etc.

Wendy's Wisdom

You may not need many of these clauses. Most transactions go smoothly or just have small bumps. These clauses are for your protection in situations where things DON'T go smoothly. Think of them kind of like a life insurance policy – you hope you never need it, but if you do, you are glad to know it's there.

Property Lines

> *If there are any undisclosed problems with boundary lines, easements, etc. that arise prior to closing on the property, the purchaser may elect to pay whatever cost may be involved in correcting these problems to the purchaser's satisfaction, and deduct the cost from the purchase price at closing.*

This clause gives you the flexibility to correct issues with easements and property boundaries if you should need to. However, there is a caveat I would add to this – if you are going to incur costs to correct these issues and deduct it from the purchase price, you need to make sure the seller has enough equity in the property to cover the costs. If they don't have enough equity, they may not be able to sell the home and satisfy their mortgage.

You may also want to consider adding this clause:

Seller agrees to provide a 1 year home warranty and will only be responsible for any deductibles.

This takes some of the financial burden of repairs off the seller's shoulders, but still gives you the protection of making sure the home can be fixed during your rental period. This is particularly useful when your seller can't afford to pay the entire repair bills.

This covers the Sales Contract. In the next chapter, we will look at the Memorandum of Option, which can be beneficial to you as the buyer. It isn't required, but it's highly recommended.

Chapter 10

Memorandum of Option

The *Memorandum of Option* is a document that gives the world notice of the option the seller is giving to you, the tenant-buyer. I do recommend that you record a Memorandum of Option at your local clerk's office, when possible, because its purpose is to protect you.

The memorandum is a recordable document that *clouds* the seller's title. This clouding means the title cannot be conveyed (transferred) or even refinanced until the memorandum is lifted. The seller cannot sell the house out from under you while your option is valid.

Wendy's Wisdom

The Memorandum of Option is NOT required in a rent-to-own transaction. As a buyer, however, it can be advantageous to you to have it because it gives you a measure of protection.

The Basics

What it Contains

These are the basic points the Memorandum of Option covers:

- When the option is valid

- Who the parties are

- Legal description and physical address of the property

- It may contain other provisions

- It needs to be notarized to be recorded

What the Memorandum of Option Does Not Contain

It does not contain the details of the transaction. It doesn't usually contain any financial numbers regarding rental amounts or purchase price.

Fill in the Blanks

The major items you need to fill in are:

- The dates of the option

- The names of the parties involved

- The physical address and legal description of the property

- Where to mail the document when it has been recorded against the title (it should be mailed back to you)

Pro-Buyer

This is really a pro-buyer document, for the most part. Once you file a memorandum on a property, the seller cannot:

- Sell to anyone else (or)

- Refinance the property

These are transactions the seller shouldn't be doing anyway during the option period. Certainly they shouldn't be selling to anyone else! Also, you don't want them refinancing because it can impact their ability to sell the home to you, particularly if they refinance and pull out some equity. This essentially keeps them honest and really isn't going to be a problem with most sellers, but it is an important purpose of the memorandum of option.

Wendy's Wisdom

This is crucial - I would not do a lease option or rent-to-own without the seller signing a Memorandum of Option.

Requirements

This is the only document that you will sign with your seller that is notarized. This document must be notarized to be recorded in all states that I am aware of. If you need a Memorandum of Option, there is one included in my Rent-to-Buy companion course, which is available on my website, www.WendyPatton.com, in the section titled "Wendy's Store".

This covers the Memorandum of Option. In the next chapter, we will look at the key points to negotiate before you complete these contracts with your seller.

PART 4:

MAKING AN OFFER AND NEGOTIATIONS

Chapter 11

Key Points to Negotiate – Not All Deals are Created Equal

Rent-to-own transactions have more terms to negotiate than most real estate transactions. While this might seem complicated, in actuality it gives you more ways to work around terms that your seller is stuck on. For instance, if your seller is fixated on a specific price, you can negotiate to your benefit in other areas to accommodate him, such as monthly option credits. If you really want the 1965 Mustang convertible in his garage, you can offer him your first born as an even exchange.

Life is all about negotiating. Think about a two year old who asks for another cookie. You tell him, *"No."* He asks again. You say, *"No."* He starts to pout and asks a third time. You answer, *"No."* Then he starts to cry. This can go on and on…what do you do? Hopefully you didn't trade him to the seller for the Mustang, no matter how tempting it was when he cried.

The world's most effective negotiating technique!

Some of us would say, *"Go to your room or sit in that corner because you are not getting another cookie."* Some of us might say, *"Fine, here is the cookie, but no more."* And some of us would say, *"Okay, you can have another cookie after your nap."* The two year old is negotiating with his parent and sometimes he wins! All of us, in some way, like to negotiate.

Many home buyers and sellers think that price and closing costs are the only negotiating points for them to buy or sell a home. There are certainly more negotiating points than price, and the more of them you know, the stronger your negotiating advantage is. We'll get into some of the HOWS of negotiating in the next chapter. Here we will focus on WHAT to negotiate.

Wendy's Wisdom

Remember, a real estate agent can help you with negotiations. Real estate agents also deal with submitting offers and counter-offers, so you don't have to negotiate face-to-face with your sellers. This gives you time to re-check this book for items to negotiate in case you forget something.

Price

Price, of course, is the big one that most everyone focuses on. In rent-to-own, sales price gets a little more complicated because the sale takes place over time. This means that the *value* of the home may *increase or decrease* during the course of the rental period, depending on your real estate market.

Rent-to-own homes often can bring higher sales prices because of the flexibility being offered to the buyer. If a seller understands rent-to-own, he will want a better price. The price premium for rent-to-own will depend on local real estate market conditions. The stronger the real estate market, the greater the premium a seller can ask for. Even if you agree to pay this price, the home must still appraise for this amount. If it doesn't appraise for enough at the end of the term, or when you are applying for your mortgage, the lender will not give you a mortgage and you won't be able to buy the home (unless the seller agrees to reduce the price). The seller doesn't have to agree to reduce the price, and if you can't get a mortgage because the appraisal isn't high enough, you would lose your option fee.

Remember in Chapter 3 when I talked about setting a budget? The price you agree to must be within your budget, no matter what the monthly rent on the home is. In some areas, the rent on a home is lower than what the mortgage payment would be, so you shouldn't base your budget just on the monthly rent and think you can afford to buy the home.

Wendy's Wisdom

Work with a mortgage broker to determine how much home you can afford. Keep to your budget when you are finding your rent-to-own home. Remember, you want to achieve the dream of homeownership, not have it become a nightmare.

If you are living in a market that is appreciating right now, the seller may want to take into account some of the market appreciation in determining the price. His home may be more valuable by the time you actually purchase it than it is right now. However, you may want to look at the flipside, too. If your market is declining, especially declining rapidly, you may want to get a lower price, despite the fact that the home is being sold as a rent-to-own. This will help take into account some of the decline in value.

You can also try to re-negotiate price at the end of the option period, particularly if the value has declined significantly. However, the seller is not obligated to come down. He is only required to sell the home based on the original terms that were set. If the home has dropped in value, what I recommend is that you show the seller the current appraisal. Explain to him that this is the current value of the house and even if he tries to sell it to someone else, he'll have to sell it according to the depreciated value. Plus, if he sells it to someone else, it will sit on the market for awhile until he finds a new buyer, which will ultimately cost him more, so he might consider selling it to you now for the new price.

You can add a purchase price in the sales contract. For instance, *"$150,000 or appraised value at the time of closing, whichever is lower (appraiser to be selected by purchaser)."* This would keep you in the home even if the appraisal went lower than the $150,000.

Selling price is typically the most important term to home sellers. Most sellers have a particular price in mind and they really don't want to budge. As long as that price is within your budget, that's okay. There are many other terms we will cover that you can negotiate to make the deal better for you.

Monthly Rent

Most sellers make the mistake of asking for the amount of their mortgage payment as the monthly rent - this is usually too high. It's a good idea to find out what the market rental rates are for your area, not just for rent-to-own homes, but for rental homes. If you are armed with this knowledge, it will help you a great deal in determining what a fair rental rate is for the home. It's always helpful if you are able to show the seller rental comparables so they can see that their rate is too high.

If the seller has to receive this amount because he can't afford to cover his mortgage payment otherwise, you can always ask for option credits to offset the difference. In this case, I would ask for the difference *plus* 50% of the difference as an incentive for paying the higher rate. It would look like this: Let's say the seller's mortgage payment is $1,450 and that is what they are asking in rent. If the area rental rate for comparable homes is $1,200, then the difference is $250. I would ask for the $250 difference plus an additional $125 in option credits, for a total of $375. However, you don't necessarily want to limit yourself to asking for $375 in option credits. You will want to tack this amount on to whatever you've already asked for in option credits when the seller indicates that they won't budge on rent.

One warning: Make sure that all of these option credits don't put the seller "upside down" with his equity. If what you end up owing him at closing is less than what he owes on his mortgage, it might be difficult for the seller to come up with the funds to pay the difference. Just keep this in mind from the beginning. Even if he says he can pay the difference today, who knows what tomorrow will bring for the seller.

Option Fee

The *Option Fee* is the amount you pay to the seller in order to have the exclusive right to buy their home. The Option Fee will be credited against the selling price when you buy, but if you don't purchase the home, the Option Fee is non-refundable. In my experience, the Option Fee is the term that tenant-buyers are most concerned about because they don't have a lot of money saved up.

Wendy's Wisdom

The lower the option fee, the less you risk losing if you don't buy the home. No matter how much you can pay now, it's usually best to pay as low an option fee as reasonably possible. If you have saved a lot of money, you can always use that as a down payment when you actually purchase the home instead of putting it down as an option fee.

No matter how much money you have saved it is to your advantage to pay as low an option fee as possible. If you don't buy the home, you lose the option fee, so the smaller the option fee the less you risk losing.

Sellers, however, like to see large option fees. This is their security for offering their home as a rent-to-own. The larger the option fee, the less likely the buyer is to walk away from it.

Wendy's Wisdom

Remember, the option fee is NOT the same as the security deposit. The security deposit is refundable to you whether you buy the home or not. The security deposit is collected as a guarantee against damages to the home and any unpaid rent. As long as the home is returned undamaged to the seller, you are entitled to the return of your security deposit. If you buy the home, you would receive your security deposit back no matter what condition the home is in. Therefore, it is always to your advantage to have more of your money put towards the security deposit than the option fee.

Option fees also depend on real estate market conditions. In strong real estate markets (one's favoring the seller); tenant-buyers can expect to pay 3% to 5% of the purchase price for their option fee. In weaker markets (one's favoring the buyer); option fees tend to run closer to 1% to 3% of the purchase price.

If your seller doesn't understand rent-to-own, he might think he has to bring the option fee to the closing to give back to you when you buy the home. This is incorrect. Instead, he will give a *payoff letter* or *a balance due letter* to the closing agent so the option fee amount can be credited.

Option Credits

Option Credits are great for tenant-buyers. They are like free money. Option credits can either come from credits on monthly rent or for credits for repairs and improvements to the home. Wherever they come from, you and the seller must agree to them in writing. The Option credits will be *deducted from the end purchase price* when you buy the home. If you don't buy the home, though, the option credits disappear. Like the option fee, you are only entitled to option credits if you buy the home.

Option credits can be structured in different ways. The simplest way is to have an amount from the monthly rental payment apply as an option credit each month, and the amount can vary to whatever you agree to.

As I mentioned, you can also use option credits for repairs and improvements to the home, particularly a fixer-upper home. They allow you to build "sweat equity." Let's say the roof of the home needs to be replaced and this is work you are comfortable doing yourself. It might normally cost the seller $3,500 to have this repair done, but you can do it yourself for around $1,000 in material cost. You can ask the seller for an option credit to replace the roof. Since it would normally cost him $3,500, you can ask for an option credit of maybe $4,000 or $4,500. Since it only costs you $1,000, you can accumulate $3,000 to $3,500 in option credits. Why would the seller give you $4,000 or more in option credits if he can have it done for $3,500? Convenience and savings. He doesn't have to arrange for the work to be done and he doesn't have to pay for it. This saves him time and keeps his money in his pockets. It's often much easier to have someone else pay for the work (you) than for them to pay for it themselves and wait until the home sells to recover their money. An additional benefit to the seller is that if you don't buy the home, he gets a free roof.

Wendy's Wisdom

If you are doing some repairs, consider having the seller pay for the materials and you do the labor. You then only get credit for the labor. If you didn't buy the home, you are only out your time - not the money and time.

The amount of monthly rent, if any, applied as option credits is entirely up to you and the seller. I have done rent-to-own deals where the entire monthly rent applies as an option credit and I have done them where none of the rent applies. You and the seller will need to reach an agreement.

Option credits can be very useful to you in two ways:

1. They can be useful in offsetting other negotiation terms with the seller, for example, meeting their asking price or their monthly rental amount

2. They are a great way to accumulate down payment funds for a mortgage; the more equity you have in the home, the better off you are when obtaining a mortgage

Length of Option

This might seem like a small thing, but it is very important. The duration of your option, meaning how long you have to buy the home before the option expires, can significantly impact whether or not you can buy the home.

If you have damaged credit, you will most likely need a minimum of 18 months to repair it. I would suggest you make the option at least 24 months to give yourself some leeway. If you are fresh off a foreclosure or bankruptcy, you'll probably need longer than that. For the most part, the longer the option period, the better for you. However, if you have too long of an option period, you may procrastinate doing credit repair and that is definitely bad. You want to start repairing your credit right away. Visit my website and click on the mortgage lender link (in the Rent-to-Own area) to determine what time frame you will need to be mortgage-ready. My lender will do this for you at no charge, usually within 24 hours. If you wish, you may consider using them to help you repair your credit during the term of the rental, then to secure your mortgage to purchase the home.

There is a potential problem for the seller with an option period that runs too long - *capital gains tax*. If the option runs too long (I won't go into the details of the Capital Gains Exclusion here) and the seller stands to make a large amount of money on the sale of his home, he could be hit with a large tax payment. This doesn't really affect you as a buyer, but it's something to keep in mind because it can help you understand why the seller may be reluctant to agree to a long option period.

Repairs

Depending on the condition of the rent-to-own home you want to buy, repairs can either be a large expense or small expense. The larger the potential expense, the more you'll want to negotiate to protect yourself on this point. The spectrum can run from having the seller pay them all to you paying them all, or you can negotiate a compromise.

If you choose to cover the repairs and improvements, you may want to ask for option credits. As we discussed before, this gives you the advantage of building up equity in the home. This is good for the seller as well, allowing him to defer the cost until the home is sold. Make sure that any agreement you reach with the seller regarding repairs, improvements and option credits is in writing.

Remember also, that you can change the wording in my contracts such that any repairs are the responsibility of the seller, and if you have to pay for the repairs yourself, the amount will be *deducted from the purchase price plus an additional amount.* Having this pre-worded into a contract makes it less likely to be an item the seller will negotiate, he may just accept that term as is.

Property Taxes

The seller should be paying the property taxes. This is an owner expense. However, should the seller fail to pay the taxes, my contracts do allow you to make the payment yourself and deduct the amount from the monthly rent (or if the amount is greater than the monthly rent, the extra amount would be deducted from the purchase price).

Special Assessments

Tax assessments levied against the rent-to-own home, such as road, sewer or lighting assessments, can be negotiated as well. Any assessments due before you actually buy the home should be paid by the seller. In some cases, there can be assessments paid in installments that extend beyond the rental period to when you purchase the home. If this is the case, you can request that all assessments be paid in full by the seller at the time of closing (this is how it is worded in my contracts). Another option is to have the assessment prorated to the time of closing. This means that the seller would be responsible for the assessment up until the day of closing, and you would be responsible for the assessment after you purchase the home.

Closing Cost Contributions

If you have never purchased a home before, you may not be aware of how substantial the costs can be (originating a mortgage, paying the closing agent, paying for title insurance, etc.). If you have bought a home before, this won't be such a shock, but it will still be financially painful. It can easily run into thousands of dollars.

Many conventional homebuyers typically ask the seller to "pay" for the buyer's closing costs. In reality the seller isn't actually paying for it, the closing costs are wrapped into the mortgage allowing you to finance them. In a rent-to-own situation, you can also ask the seller to pay for your closing costs, or part of your closing costs in this manner.

I'm not wild about the idea of including your closing costs in the mortgage if you can avoid it. You are essentially financing up-front costs and then paying interest on them for a very long period of time. The end result is that if you lived in the home for 30 years until it was paid off, you would end up paying approximately two to three times the amount of the original closing costs in interest. That may be why banks are happy to let you finance your closing costs - because they make more money.

There is a trade-off with paying closing costs up front. You will have less money as a down payment against the home. Typically, the larger the down payment you have, the lower your interest rate on the mortgage will be. Even a difference as little as ¼ of a percentage point in lower interest can save you thousands of dollars over the life of a mortgage. For example, if you have a 30-year mortgage for $150,000 at 6.5% interest, you'll pay about $191,000 in interest. If you have the same $150,000 mortgage at

6.25% interest, you'll pay about $182,500 in interest. That's a savings of $8,500, which could be more than you would pay in closing costs.

Probably the best way to determine if you should pay closing costs or increase your down payment when buying the home is to talk to your mortgage broker and see if increasing the down payment will reduce your interest rate, and by how much.

Closing Costs

In addition to you, the buyer, having to pay closing costs, the seller also has to pay for things such as title insurance, and in some states, deed revenue stamps (a.k.a. Transfer of Deed Fee). These costs are not normally negotiated; they are just something the seller pays. It is important to be aware of these costs in the unlikely event the seller tries to ask you to pay for part of them.

Security Deposit

Sellers may or may not want or ask for a security deposit. As I said earlier, it is to your advantage to have more money down as a security deposit than an option fee because the security deposit is refundable if you don't buy the home. Keep in mind, however, that many sellers want to see a bigger option fee and if you offer too low of an option fee, they may not want to sell you their home on a rent-to-own.

Homeowners Association (HOA)

Homeowners Association Fees or dues (HOA) should be paid by the seller during the rental period. During the rental period, you are still only a tenant, so you shouldn't be paying owner expenses like HOA and property taxes.

Household Maintenance

Every home has a variety of regular maintenance requirements: Mowing the lawn, maintaining the landscaping, snow shoveling, well and septic care, pool cleaning, water softener, and so on. If you have to pay professionals to maintain all of these, the costs can really add up! Some of them, like lawn mowing and snow shoveling are things you can easily do yourself. This would be standard for renters and future homeowners (yes, this is you!). Other services, like the well and septic maintenance, have to be done by professionals and should be included in your rental agreement as to who is responsible for these items or you may end up paying for them whether you wanted to or not!

Items Within the Home

Any items that will be included in the purchase of your rent-to-own home, such as the refrigerator, stove, dishwasher, washer, dryer, pool table, cast iron stove, etc. all have value. Many times sellers have already written off these things in their mind as just included with the home, particularly the appliances. This is good for you as a buyer because it means you are essentially getting them for free.

Sometimes sellers have emotional attachment to these items and either want to take them or want more for them than they are really worth. It's important to keep this in mind as you negotiate. If you ask the seller to include the cast iron stove and they want an extra $2,000 for the purchase price to do it, you need to recognize that the numbers are out of whack. No matter how much you might love that stove and want it in the house, it is simply not worth that much money! The same thing goes for the appliances. It can be a nice convenience factor to have the appliances included with the home, but if the seller is asking too much money for used appliances, it just isn't worth it.

A good way to get the seller to reconsider is to point out the actual value of the used item. Then add the cost to the seller to move that item out of the home and that gives you a final value, which is probably a lot less than they were asking.

Anything Else Between the Buyer and the Seller

You can negotiate and add almost anything you want into a Sales Contract. The occupancy date, how issues from the home inspection will be handled, and so on.

Wendy's Wisdom

Does this seem like too much to keep track of? If you use my contracts, many of these points are already worded into the contract for the seller to pay, such as property taxes or assessments. Other items like repairs can be worded the way you want (pro-buyer) in your initial offer. Many times, the seller will just accept it without negotiation. Remember, my contracts are available at www.Wendy Patton.com.

As you can see, if you add up all the different negotiation points, they can be worth tens of thousands of dollars. Ignoring a little thing here or there may cost you a lot of money. Certainly, some of them you don't necessarily want to mention if the seller doesn't bring them up. Leave the wording in the contracts for things like property taxes or assessments and then let the seller try to negotiate them away if they don't want to pay for them.

Presenting the Offer

A good thing about being the buyer is that you are in the position of making the initial offer. This is very advantageous for you. Why? Because it means you (or your real estate agent) will submit the offer with all of the paperwork already created. You can submit your offer with a copy of *the Sales Contract, the Option Agreement, the Rental Agreement and the Memorandum of Option*. By making that initial offer, you will use the contracts YOU choose instead of the seller's contracts. This allows you to use pro-buyer contracts.

I'm going to give you an example of an initial offer so you can see how all of the terms I talked about previously would be covered. Let's say that you are looking at a home that is for sale as a rent-to-own with an asking price of $160,000, a monthly rent of $1,300 and an option fee of 2.5% (or $4,000). This is what your initial offer might look like (it is totally up to you what you offer for your rent-to-own home purchase, this is just an example):

1. **Purchase Price** - $155,000. This goes into the Sales Contract. In many cases, sellers do not expect to receive their full asking price, particularly in soft real estate markets. Even as a rent-to-own, you can offer less than the full asking price. Remember, the seller isn't going to negotiate down, they'll be going up so you want to start with something that gives you room to negotiate. In many cases, it pays to not go too low with the purchase price because it's the first thing sellers look at in an offer. You can effectively lower the purchase price by increasing the option credits and it won't appear as bad to the seller.

2. **Monthly Rent** - $1,300. This goes into the Rental Agreement. I'm keeping the monthly rent the same as what they are asking, but I'll be making up for it when I ask for option credits below.

3. **Option Fee** – 1% or $1,550. You'll put this amount in the Option Agreement.

4. **Option Credits** - $1,000 per month. This also goes into the Option Agreement. Over a 24 month option period, that would amount to $24,000. See how I effectively lowered the purchase price and offset the $1,300 monthly rent. You may not get the full amount in option credits, but it's good to give yourself plenty of room to negotiate with this.

5. **Length of Option** – 30 months. This would be written into the Option Agreement as well. You would actually write in the date the option would expire (30 months from now) instead of writing in the length of the option. By asking for 30 months, I'm giving myself an entire year more than I should need and hopefully can settle at 6 months less, or 24 months. This will give me 6 months of wiggle room.

6. **Repairs** – Seller pays. This would be in the Rental Agreement. If you have this clause typed as though it's part of the contract versus hand writing it in, you are less likely to even need to negotiate this. When dealing with contracts, people are more likely to focus on and negotiate over things that are hand written.

7. **Property Taxes** – Seller pays until purchase. This would go in the Sales Contract and there should already be a clause indicating the taxes will be prorated to the date of sale.

8. **Special Assessments** – Seller pays. Again, this goes in the Sales Contract and should be a pre-printed clause. Any assessments that exist before the date of sale would be the seller's responsibility.

9. **Closing Cost Contributions** – Seller to pay up to 2% of the purchase price towards buyer's closing costs. This would be written into the Sales Contract as an additional condition. Closing cost contributions are typically expressed as a percentage of the purchase price. Do talk to a lender to see what the standard practice is in your area at the time you are making an offer.

10. **Closing Costs** – Seller will pay all of their closing costs. This is just standard. The only time you would need to change this is if the seller writes in something different.

11. **Security Deposit** - $1,300. Put this in the Rental Agreement. In regular rentals, security deposits often are one month's rent. I'm borrowing that standard here and increasing my security deposit so I can keep the option fee down.

12. **HOA** – Seller pays. This would appear in the Sales Contract. If it isn't pre-printed, you can just write in the *additional conditions* section that the HOA (if there is

one) will be prorated to the date of closing. This makes the seller responsible during the rental period.

13. **Household Maintenance** – Buyer pays except for certain things. This would appear in the Rental Agreement. This refers to basic maintenance you would do to maintain the home like mowing the lawn or shoveling the snow. Special maintenance items like well and septic maintenance would have their own clause and you would want to pre-print that the seller is responsible for these items during the rental period.

14. **Items Within the Home** – Refrigerator, stove, dishwasher, washer, dryer and hot tub. This goes into the Sales Contract.

This is how the terms in the initial offer would be handled. A number of them are already pre-printed so they are less likely to be negotiated by the seller. In this example, we gave the seller close to the asking price and their monthly rent because we were making up for it in other places.

If you are working with a real estate agent, they will help you with all of these things. They are very experienced at completing these contracts. You may also want to reference this chapter as you are completing your initial offer.

Now that you know the items you can include in your negotiations, let's take a look at some tips and tricks of HOW to negotiate in the next chapter.

Chapter 12

Negotiating Tips

It would be great if negotiating real estate deals could be done by passing the peace pipe!

You don't need to be an expert negotiator to negotiate successfully. It wouldn't be possible for me to teach you to be an expert negotiator in one chapter anyway. The point of this chapter is to teach you some useful tips and tricks to help you negotiate better. The reason we need to know how to negotiate is that everyone (including you and the seller) likes to negotiate to some extent.

Let me give you an example:

You make an offer on a rent-to-own home - an offer that you think is a good starting point for negotiations. After you submit the offer, the seller accepts it, every single part of it, without change. How do you feel? Bad, right? As though you made your offer too high. Even if you thought it was good for you initially, after the seller accepted it, you felt like you should have asked for more - even though you got everything you wanted. It's crazy, I know, but our perceptions can change that easily. If the seller had negotiated with you on just one small item, like the occupancy date (when you could move in), you would have felt better. It's a strange world we live in where if we get everything we want without effort, we aren't happy with it.

When you combine these tips and tricks with the knowledge of what to negotiate (from Chapter 11), you will be better prepared to negotiate effectively for the purchase of your rent-to-own home.

Wendy's Wisdom

Remember, your real estate agent can help you with negotiations.

The average tenant-buyer doesn't negotiate very much. They usually accept all of the seller's terms except the option fee (they'll usually try to negotiate this). My goal is to make you a better negotiator than the average tenant-buyer. You can get a much better deal if you just ask for it and that can save you thousands of dollars.

Negotiating Techniques: Keep Your Eye on the Prize

I'm stealing this phrase from sports, but it applies here as well. This is important for three reasons:

1. It will keep your negotiations on track. Your main goal is to buy a rent-to-own home. If you keep this in mind while you negotiate, it will help ensure that you negotiate towards that goal.

2. By remembering what your ultimate goal is, you will stop yourself from negotiating the deal to death. If your seller is only doing light negotiations and you pull out the horse blankets to haggle over every little, itty-bitty detail, you'll kill the deal. The sellers will turn you down and find another buyer.

3. If negotiations are intense and you start getting stuck on really small points, you'll lose out on the big picture. You want to buy a rent-to-own home. In the end, it really doesn't matter too much if you concede a couple of small points, if you still achieve your end goal.

While I strongly recommend keeping your eye on your main goal, I don't recommend that you let your sellers walk all over you in the negotiations. It's okay to concede a few little sticking points if it will get the deal done. If you give in to everything just to find a rent-to-own home, it will end up being a lousy deal for you. Also, if the seller had such an easy time with the negotiations, they'll probably keep walking all over you while you are a tenant.

Ask Questions

You'll want to do this both before and during negotiations. The purpose is to understand what the seller's core motivation is. Why are they selling their home? Once you understand their motivation, you can tailor your negotiations towards meeting that need. If you can meet their core motivation (for example, the husband and wife have recently married and they now own two homes and are stuck with two mortgage payments), you'll find that it will be much easier to negotiate when you can reassure them that soon they'll no longer be saddled with that extra mortgage payment. This will make it much easier for you to negotiate on points that are important to you.

When you ask questions, practice silence after your question. Let them talk and listen for clues. You will learn a lot more if you zip it and let them talk.

They typically won't tell you their core need immediately. By listening, you can start to get a better understanding and then can ask a more specific question and use silence again. It usually takes three similar questions before they'll give you their core need. For example, you might start with the question, *"So why are you selling your home?"* In their answer they might say something like, *"It seemed like the right time."* Not too specific. You can respond by saying, *"Oh, did something change to make you want to sell your home?"* Then they may say, *"Well, we just got married."* Then you can ask, *"So you both owned a home before you got married?"*

You want to ask them open-ended questions to give them room to talk and give you details. Try not to ask a question that requires a yes or no answer. You can learn a lot by their answers.

Don't Give Away Anything without Asking for Something in Return

This tit-for-tat technique helps ensure that even if you are giving your sellers a key aspect that they want; you are getting something in return. A good way to handle this is with a question, *"If I agree to your asking price, how much per month in option credits do you think is a fair exchange?"*

Or, you can ask for exactly what you want, *"If I agree to your asking price, would you agree to give me $1,000 per month in option credits?"*

By asking a question, you give the seller a chance to voice what they think is a fair exchange for what they are asking for. It may turn out to be MORE than what you would have asked for. If it isn't enough, you can always negotiate up from their proposal.

By stating what you want, you are more limited. The seller may even try to negotiate you down from this position. However, if there are a few key things that you really want out of the negotiation, this is a good time to go after them.

Make Your Concessions Progressively Smaller

A lot of people make the mistake of keeping their concessions even over the course of negotiations. What you really want to do is to concede smaller and smaller amounts each time. Let me give you an example to illustrate what I mean.

Suppose you make an initial offer of $140,000 on a home with a $150,000 asking price. The seller counters back at $148,000. So you come up to $145,000 and then the seller counters at $147,000. So you come up to $146,500.

What if you did this instead? You offer $140,000 initially and when the seller counters at $148,000 you talk to them, focusing on how bad the market is and grudgingly come up to $142,000. They counter back at $145,000. You then explain to them that by working with you, they'll get this mortgage payment taken care of so they won't have to worry about it anymore. You'd be willing to come up to $143,000. Now, they counter back at $144,000. You say, *"We're getting close. If you come down to $143,500, I think we'll have a deal."* Do you see how in the second example each counter was smaller and for progressively less money? In both examples, you countered back three times. However, the end result of the first example was $146,500 and the second was $143,500, a difference of $3,000. Three grand may not sound like a whole lot when you are talking about a $150,000 home, but think instead of what an extra $3,000 could buy you in savings.

Just a few ideas of how you might spend your extra $3,000. ☺

Silence is Golden - Get the Gold

This is one of my favorites, but the hardest for me to do personally. You can use it either after a seller makes a counter offer on a negotiating point or after you ask a question about their counter.

Once you choose silence, you must wait until the seller responds. Don't be the first one to break the silence.

People aren't comfortable with silence. The longer it drags out, the more uncomfortable they'll become. Once they say something, it will be more than likely that their position won't be as strong. I am not sure why this works, but I assume most people are like me and they feel they need to say something when there is silence. If they make a counter offer and you just stare back at them, they'll begin to think that it wasn't very realistic. When they break the silence, they may revise their offer upward. Even if they don't revise it up right away, they will likely be more amenable to your progressively smaller counter offers.

If you respond to their counter offer with a question and then silence, for example, *"You are offering me $250 a month in option credits?"* they will likely revise that amount upwards before you even have to make a counter to their offer. For example, they might blurt out, *"Well, we could go up to $400."*

Handling Road Blocks

Sometimes negotiations get stuck. You hit a point with your seller that neither of you are willing to concede. Usually this happens when you have both lost perspective and it becomes more important to win on that one point than to achieve your overall goal, which in your case is to buy a rent-to-own home. If you get stuck in your negotiations, there are several things you can do to keep things moving along:

- *Try a fresh approach.* Either change your scenery (go out with your seller for a cup of coffee and continue talking there) or try to look at the issue from a new angle. Basically, you want to try to give your mind a fresh perspective on the issue.

- *Move on to something else.* It can help to table the point and continue on to other negotiating items. Once you have worked out other details, you may not find that particular point to be such a stickler.

- *Use a conditional concession.* Try the question, *"If I do this X, would you do this Y?"* In this case, you are saying that you are willing to give up a concession if your seller is willing to give on something in return. By phrasing it in the form of a question, you are indicating that you won't give it up without the seller giving in on something as well.

Wince

In fact, a large portion of negotiations is non-verbal communication. Body language plays a big part by sending s*ignals.* They can range from subtle nods of the head to the closed mind of arms being crossed. The wince is one of the most effective forms of body language. A well-used wince following a counter offer from the seller can convey volumes of information without you having to say anything. It indicates that their offer is not acceptable and, not only is it not acceptable; it is almost painfully not acceptable.

A wince followed by stony silence can be very effective at getting the seller to up the ante without you having to say a word.

You can also follow the wince with a question, *"Is that the best you can do?"*

Either way, the intent is to get the seller to either revise their counter offer downward or at least, mentally plant the thought that they are not conceding enough.

Location of Negotiation

Whenever possible, you want to be the one selecting the location for your negotiations. Remember back in Chapter 3, I talked about the emotions of home buying? Well, if you are making an offer to the sellers and are staring out the window at that swimming pool you fell in love with, how strong do you think you'll negotiate? The answer is: not very. You'll do whatever it takes to get the home because your emotions are controlling your negotiations.

You might be better off meeting with the seller on neutral ground to make your offer. This will help you keep your mind focused on buying the rent-to-own home without being so emotionally attached to it.

Wendy's Wisdom

If you are working with a real estate agent, you won't be meeting with the seller in person to make your offer. Your offer will be submitted through the agent. This way you don't have to worry about the location of negotiation.

If You Don't Ask – The Answer is Always "No"

This is a pretty simple rule. If there is something you want in the negotiations, you'll never get it if you don't ask for it. You may not get it even if you DO ask for it, or you may only get part of it (whatever IT is, like the eBay commercials), but you must ask to have any chance of getting it. Remember, the worst they can say is "no". If you don't ask, the answer is always "no".

The Alternative

The alternative is when you have another house as a choice. You mention the other house to the seller during the negotiation to let them know that their home isn't your only choice. It plants the seed in the seller's mind that if you aren't happy with the deal offered on their home, you may choose to purchase the other home. The purpose is to help motivate the seller to make concessions.

In reality, this alternative may or may not exist. It is definitely to your benefit to know what else is out there, whether you are really interested in it or not, just for the sake of having the information to leverage against the seller. Your real estate agent can help you with this by providing you with comparable listings.

Don't Get Desperate

Depending on your real estate market, there may not be many rent-to-own homes available. If this is the case, you may feel some urgency to get this particular rent-to-own home because it's your best option. If you start to feel desperate, you will begin making bad decisions and give away WAY too much in the negotiations. If you *are* desperate – try to keep it to yourself (don't even share it completely with your real estate agent).

You definitely don't want to let on to the seller that you need to buy their home urgently. That's the same as asking them to take shameless advantage of you.

Here is a good point to keep in mind if you start feeling desperate: If it starts to look like the deal is falling apart, instead of giving away a bunch of concessions to save it, focus on reiterating to the seller how their needs are being met. If you asked questions and listened earlier, you should have a good idea of what your seller's core needs are and you'll want to bring those back up.

Ways to Counter

Sellers also have negotiating tricks they may try to use on you. If you are prepared ahead of time, you'll have little problem responding to them if they come up during the negotiations.

The Take-Away

Once you have become attached to a home, it can be hard to let it go. A seller can use this to their advantage by threatening to pull the deal. They might say something like, *"You know I don't think my house is right for you. Maybe you should consider another one."*

The purpose is to effectively halt negotiations and get you to say, *"No, I really do want this home."* The take-away can be particularly effective with tenant-buyers who have few or no alternatives. If there are a lot of rent-to-own homes available in your area, you can make the take-away backfire by saying, *"You know, I think you are right. I think we'll go have another look at some other homes."*

If you really do want the seller's home and they try the take-away, you can counter it by saying something like, *"Well, I may have to consider another home if you aren't more willing to negotiate. What you need to ask yourself is do you want to sell your home or do you want it to keep sitting on the market?"* You are effectively reversing the take-away on the seller.

Last Minute Add On

This trick is used to try to capture small concessions at the last minute after everything else has been agreed upon. The idea is that once you are already emotionally invested in the deal, you don't want to let it go over just a couple of little things thrown in at the last minute.

There are a couple of effective ways to counter this technique:

- *Say "No"*. At this point, the seller is likely just as emotionally invested in the deal as you are and isn't going to walk away from it if you won't give in on these last minute requests. Hopefully, you also have everything in writing and signed.

- *Counter by asking for something in return*. This is the tit-for-tat technique that will allow you to meet their last minute request if they are willing to give up something in return.

You can also use this technique to your advantage. For instance, if you want to move in a few days early or get a jump start on painting before you move in, you can use the last minute add on to try to get them to agree.

Questions

Sellers may use questions to try to determine what your core motivation is, too. It's a lot easier for them to negotiate with you if you give away too much information.

The best ways to handle their questions are to either answer their question with a question, ask them to repeat their question, or to explain what they mean; or you can answer a different question. The intent is to keep them talking and also not give away too much personal information.

Silence

A seller may try to use silence with you either after you make an offer or after asking you a question. If they use silence after you make an offer, the best way to counter it is with silence yourself. You've had your say, just wait for them to respond.

If they use silence after asking you a question, ask them to explain what they meant. Get them talking again to prevent them from using this technique.

The Wince...at You

The best way to handle someone wincing at you is to ignore it. If they wince, you can act like it didn't happen and continue on with what you are saying.

Another option is to respond with a question, *"Well, what do you think?"* or *"Are you interested in my offer?"* Or, you can even hit it straight on and say, *"You didn't seem to like that, why?"*

Shouting

Shouting is an intimidation technique designed to put you off guard and make you feel as though you've really upset the other party. It is intended to be a power shift. If the seller shouts in response to your offer something like, *"You'll have to do better than that!"* you can respond to their outburst either with silence or by repeating what they said in the form of a question, *"I'll have to do better than that?"* If you choose silence, just stare at them until they explain more clearly what they mean. This will help prevent you from giving away additional concessions without really knowing what they are looking for.

If you choose to repeat what they say in the form of a question, you are asking them to explain themselves and clarify what they mean. Either way, you want them to be more specific about what they are looking for and to stop shouting.

You may also want to think twice about buying a home from a seller that is shouting at you. If they are shouting at you when you make an offer, think about what it will be like when you are a tenant. They won't be any easier to work with then either.

Wendy's Wisdom

In most cases, you and the seller would be working with real estate agents, so you won't need to directly negotiate with the seller.

In the next chapter, we look at qualifying a seller. This is an essential step to buying your rent-to-own home and having some peace of mind.

Chapter 13

Buyers – Qualifying Sellers

I am sure you are thinking, "A seller is qualified if he has a house to sell me as a rent-to-own, right?" Or, "What the heck does it mean to qualify a seller?" Qualifying a seller means that you are making sure the seller can actually sell you that rent-to-own home.

"Why would I qualify the seller? The seller should be qualifying me." Yes, the seller should qualify you when they take a rental application. They'll verify your employment, do a background check and pull your credit. But you should also qualify them to make sure they'll be able to sell you the home. It's pretty rare that problems would come up, but in some cases there are sellers who don't know they have an issue that would keep them from selling their home and there are a few sellers who are unethical. Like I said, it's pretty rare, but it's definitely something you want to do to protect yourself.

The following is a checklist of seller qualifications. I will go over each one in detail.

1. Make sure their mortgage payment is current
2. Verify that the seller is not in financial trouble
3. Run the seller's credit
4. Pull their title work

Make Sure Their Mortgage Payment is Current

If a seller is behind on payments, they are in financial trouble. Those back payments must be caught up somehow or the lender will foreclose. Even if they start making regular payments out of your rental payment, they will still have those back payments to catch up. The lender is not going to let them sell the home until they do, and the lender may choose to foreclose at any time.

If the seller is in the situation where they are behind on payments, it doesn't automatically prevent you from being able to do a rent-to-own with them. It might still work in certain circumstances. But, somehow the seller's mortgage must be brought current. First, your option fee would have to be enough to bring the seller's mortgage back to current. If you and the seller are working with real estate agents, they will probably be taking part of that option fee as a partial commission so there might not be too much left to apply. If there isn't enough money in the option fee and the seller doesn't have the money, it probably isn't going to work.

If the seller's mortgage is brought current (you would definitely require written verification be provided to you), then the next step is making sure that the mortgage payments during the rental period are being paid. This is not something you'll want to trust the seller with given that they were already behind. You will want to make the mortgage payments directly to the lender and provide the seller with proof of payment. I'll talk more about this in Chapter 16.

The second catch with a seller who is behind on payments is that you have to make sure your rental payment is enough to cover the mortgage. If it isn't enough, then the seller would have to cover that difference. In this situation where the seller was already behind on payments, you would want to be very cautious about getting into an arrangement where the seller has to cover part of the mortgage because the rental amount isn't enough. They were already in trouble once, how can you be sure that they'll cover the difference?

You might still be able to make it work under two conditions. First, you would need to be able to comfortably afford to pay that extra yourself if the seller doesn't. If you are paying that extra, you would definitely want it deducted from the purchase price, plus interest. That being the case, you would need to make sure the seller has enough equity in their home to be able to credit you for those extra payments.

Wendy's Wisdom

In most cases, I don't really advise you to try to do a rent-to-own with a seller that is behind on their mortgage. It increases the risk for you.

To verify a seller is current on their mortgage you'll want to use this bank **Authorization to Release** letter. The seller will need to sign it in order for the bank to release this information to you.

YOUR NAME
STREET ADDRESS
CITY, STATE, ZIP
TELEPHONE NUMBER

Date

To Whom It May Concern

I, Seller's name – 1 or 2 names, give your name, the right to have access to all information regarding my mortgage with you. My mortgage loan number is their loan number.

This would include, but not limited to, checking on balances, changing the address for payment coupons and correspondence, payoff requests, etc.
Sincerely,

Owner's Signature

(Notary is recommended)

Verify That the Seller is Not in Financial Trouble

Even if a seller is current on their mortgage but is in financial trouble in other areas of their life, it can have an impact on their ability to sell you their home. If they were to declare bankruptcy, it could tie up their home, preventing you from buying it or they might be tempted to use the rent money to pay other bills instead of the mortgage payment (You could have "knee-cappers" working for the seller's bookie showing up at your door in the middle of the night looking for the seller. Okay, just kidding on that last one).

A good way to start finding out if the seller is in financial trouble is to find out where they are moving next. If they are moving back in with their parents, it is definitely not a good sign. If they are moving in with their children, that might be okay if they are retired. If they already have another home, that is usually good – as long as they are current on both of their mortgages.

Run the Seller's Credit

This goes hand-in-hand with verifying that the seller is not in financial trouble. You won't be able to pull the seller's credit report, in some cases, because the seller may not agree to it. However, if you can, it is to your benefit so you know that the seller isn't going to disappear with your money. If you can't pull their credit, you might instead require the seller to provide proof that their credit is in good shape. This isn't something that I normally do, but it is definitely worth considering as a measure of protection for you.

You won't be able to pull their credit yourself. Your mortgage broker can assist you with this. Even if you could pull their credit yourself you would most likely need your mortgage broker's help in interpreting the credit report. While credit reports aren't quite as hard as reading ancient Sanskrit, they can be difficult.

Pull Their Title Work

Title work is what tells us if the seller can sell their home, or more specifically, what restrictions the seller has on selling their home. For example, if the seller has a mortgage on the property, when the title work is pulled, it will show that there is a mortgage that would have to be paid off in order to sell the home. If the seller has unpaid property taxes, contractor liens or unpaid HOA dues, these would all likely show up on the title work. Title work will also show if someone else has a claim to the property that would prevent the seller from selling it. Once you sign all of the paperwork with your seller and record the Memorandum of Option, it would show up on the title work. The memorandum will prevent the seller from selling their home to anyone else beside you as long as the memorandum is valid.

You will need to have a title company or a title attorney (depending on what state you live in) pull title work for you. This is not something you can or should try to do on your own. The title agent can research the seller's title to verify that it is in sellable condition.

In some cases, the seller may have a "cloud" on their title. A cloud means that there is something blocking the home from being sold until the cloud is removed, such as your Memorandum of Option. This is another advantage of pulling title work early. In addition to verifying the seller can actually sell their home, it can identify possible problems that the seller can resolve. Not all clouds on the title should make you run screaming in the other direction. Some of them can be resolved during the rental period and you can still go ahead with the rent-to-own. For example, let's say the seller refinanced their home two years ago but the old lender never released the mortgage off the title. Clearly that lender isn't still owed any money since they were paid off at the refinance, but it can take a little time for the seller to go through the steps to get that old mortgage off the title. It's much better to do this research while you are renting than to find this out once you are ready to buy.

No Guarantees

Even if you take all of the above precautionary steps before you sign all of the paperwork with the seller, none of it absolutely guarantees during the rental period or even when it comes time to buy that a problem might not come up. The odds are slim, and definitely much slimmer if you take the proper precautions we just talked about, but I would be remiss if I didn't tell you that there is always a possibility that things can go wrong.

While the seller might not be in financial trouble when you start your lease, it is always possible for them to get into trouble while you are renting the home. The bank authorization letter above is crucial for you. As long as you have submitted this letter to the lender, you can periodically check on the status of the mortgage, which I recommend you do.

Wendy's Wisdom

Use the bank authorization letter! This protects you, allowing you to check on the seller's mortgage and make sure it is getting paid.

Chapter 14

Home Inspections

Home inspectors are professionals that you would hire to perform an inspection on the home you wish to buy. Their job is to examine the home, both inside and out, and assess the condition of the home and its components. They should help you identify things like whether the foundation is in danger of being carried off by ants or if there is mold in the attic. They might also determine whether there are problems with the furnace, roof, plumbing, electrical, and so on. If you have ever bought a home before, you may have worked with a home inspector.

Why a Home Inspection

Why would you need a home inspection if you'll be living in the home as a rental before you buy? Renting should give you plenty of time to find any problems before you buy, right? And, you'll save money by not having to pay for the home inspection, right? Definitely <u>not</u> <u>right</u>! I strongly encourage ALL buyers to have a home inspection done BEFORE they move in. Buying a home blind is extremely risky. Even with a rent-to-own home, you are putting your option fee at risk if you don't have a home inspection done. Also, issues like mold might not be found without an inspection.

The Sales Contract you sign should have a provision for home inspections stating the deadline for completing the home inspection and how issues arising from the inspection will be handled. If you don't have a home inspection, you are saying that you accept the home in an "as-is" condition. That means any defects; problems and corpses in the cellar are acceptable in their present condition without renegotiating. I'm just kidding about the dead animals. I have never, in all my years, found any dead animals in homes, although I have found a few "skeletons in the closet" ☺ (it is amazing what personal items home sellers neglect to put away before showings)!

By having a home inspector examine the home <u>before</u> you move in and identify potential problems or defects in the home, you are in a position to:

1. Have the seller correct the problems
2. Renegotiate the purchase price or other terms, taking the cost of those defects into account
3. Negotiate option credits by handling the repairs yourself

You can decide what is best for you, or you may select a combination of the three. It will depend on your situation.

Differences in Home Inspectors

Before I talk about where to find a home inspector, I want to talk a little about how home inspectors can vary. More than half of all states in the U.S. have NO licensing or a certification requirement, which means in many states, any Joe with a flashlight can hang out a sign and call himself a home inspector. Home inspectors are not all trained in one central location or trained with a certain set of training criteria. There is no national certification or skill level requirement for home inspectors. It is all handled on the state level.

As you can imagine, this means that not all home inspectors are created equal. There are some truly great home inspectors and there are some truly lousy ones. I have worked with both.

Before you go running the other way or throw your hands up and say "why bother", let me assure you that it is definitely possible to separate the wheat from the chaff when it comes to home inspectors. I will be giving you some great tips on finding good ones, so don't worry.

The first big difference between home inspectors is the ones that call themselves "Realtor® friendly". These guys drive me nuts. A "Realtor® friendly" home inspector is one who will perform an inspection without scaring the buyer away and killing the deal. Meaning that no matter what condition the house is in, he'll do the inspection in such a way that the buyer still feels comfortable enough to buy the home.

But wait a minute... YOU are the one hiring the home inspector. YOU are the one PAYING the home inspector. Shouldn't their responsibility be to you, the buyer, and not to the real estate agent by promising not to kill the deal? YES! "Realtor® friendly" home inspectors are nothing but a conflict of interest.

Wendy's Wisdom

Finding a Home Inspector Tip #1 – Don't use a "Realtor® friendly" home inspector. If you ask your real estate agent for a home inspector referral, make sure you specify that you want one who does not claim to be "Realtor® friendly".

Another type of home inspector that drives me crazy is the one who arrives early, before the buyer, to get a jump start on the inspection. Why would they do this? There are two reasons that come to mind:

1. They don't want the buyer to see what a shoddy inspection job they are doing

2. They don't want to answer the buyer's questions as they go through the home

Either way, it spells a lousy inspection. A good home inspector will take the time to do the inspection with the buyer present from start to finish. They will point out defects to the buyer as they see them, answer questions and explain remedies or repairs needed. You <u>want</u> to be there. This is how you learn about the home.

Wendy's Wisdom

Finding a Home Inspector Tip #2 – A good inspector will do the entire inspection with the buyer present. They will answer questions and point out problems as they go (in addition to providing you with an inspection report at the end).

ASHI

As I said, there is no national certification or standards for home inspectors. There are, however, some professional trade organizations for home inspectors. Some trade organization memberships are only worth the paper they are written on, while others are much more selective in their membership requirements.

One of the best home inspector trade organizations out there is the American Society of Home Inspectors (ASHI). The base requirements for an ASHI member are that they must have:

1. "Completed 50 home inspections and had a sampling of 5 inspections verified to be in substantial compliance with the ASHI Standards of Practice,
2. Pass the National Home Inspector Examination, and

3. Pass the ASHI Standards of Practice and Code of Ethics education module."

ASHI takes membership a step further, however, and has another level, the ASHI Certified Inspector. These inspectors have performed 250 inspections. The ASHI Certified Inspector can use the ASHI logo with "ASHI Certified Inspector" on it.

Interview Your Home Inspector

Before you select your home inspector you should ask them a few questions. Think of it as a job interview. Depending on how they answer your questions, you can decide whether or not you want to give them the job. If a potential inspector gets impatient with you or doesn't want to answer some of your questions, you can guess what type of inspector they'll be. Toss their name out and move on to the next one. If an inspector is legit and proud of his trade memberships and the quality of his work, it will show through as you interview. This is the type of inspector you want to be working with.

www.Realtor.org has a good list of 10 questions to ask a home inspector before you agree to hire one at www.realtor.org/toolkits/consumer03. The list is free and I strongly encourage you to make use of it. If you don't like an inspector's answers or the way the inspector answers the questions, move on to another one. There are plenty out there.

The Inspection

Once the home inspector has finished, given you the inspection report, gone over all of the potential and actual problems and discussed the overall condition of the home with you, you'll need to decide how to proceed. The worst case scenario, you may want to turn and run away screaming from the house. Yes, there are some bad houses out there. I actually had a home under contract once where the inspector told me "Run. Run very fast." Needless to say, I didn't buy that house.

In most cases, however, the inspection will turn up some issues, but nothing so severe that you can't work out a solution with the seller. There will always be something. If you do choose to continue with the rent-to-own purchase, you'll need to work out a solution to those issues with the seller. As I said, you have three choices:

1. Have the seller correct those problems

2. Renegotiate the purchase price or other terms, taking the cost of those defects into account

3. Negotiate option credits by handling the repairs yourself

Once you have selected a home inspector, you will schedule the inspection. I'm not going to go into details about everything an inspector will look for. The purpose here isn't to make you an expert on home inspections; after all, that's why you are hiring an inspector in the first place. If you want to know more about what home inspections typically cover go to: www.realtor.org/toolkits/consumer04.

Inspections can open up another round of negotiations based on the results of the inspection report.

Wendy's Wisdom

Look at the inspection report objectively. Now that you know more about the condition of the home, the terms of the deal may need to change. Remember to not let yourself get so emotionally attached to the home that you ignore the inspection report.

Home Warranty

No matter who is responsible for repairs during the rental period, it's a very good idea to have the seller obtain a home warranty. It offers a measure of protection for both you and the seller.

Home warranties are different from home insurance. They typically cover many repairs and replacements of things that insurance would not cover. Appliances, furnaces, water heaters and air conditioners are just a few of the things a home warranty covers.

While you might stipulate that repairs are the responsibility of the seller in your contracts, home warranties are great protection from having repairs be budget busters. For example, what if the water heater quits while you are renting the home? While the seller might be responsible for the repair, it still isn't cheap. What if the seller can't afford to replace the water heater? You certainly don't want to live in a home without hot water, so you would have to cough up the money for it yourself (which would later be deducted from the purchase price).

A much safer solution is the home warranty. If the water heater quits, the home warranty should cover it and the seller will only have to pay the deductible. This is much more affordable for the seller and gives you peace of mind knowing that you aren't going to have to pick up the tab if the seller can't afford it.

To require the seller to provide a home warranty, add it in the Sales Contract. Under *additional conditions,* write in a clause that says something like: *"Seller to provide a home warranty during the rental period."*

Fair Housing Law is next. This law is designed to protect you; to keep sellers from discriminating against you based on any protected classes. We'll look at what sellers can and can't do and steps you can take if you feel you've been discriminated against.

Chapter 15

Fair Housing Law

"Sorry, but I don't rent to someone of your skin color."

He said *what*? It's hard to believe that the Fair Housing Act was passed over 40 years ago, yet there are still landlords and sellers that discriminate against other human beings.

U.S. Department of Housing and Urban Development:

"Title VIII of the Civil Rights Act of 1968 (Fair Housing Act), as amended, prohibits discrimination in the sale, rental, and financing of dwellings, and in other housing-related transactions, based on race, color, national origin, religion, sex, familial status (including children under the age of 18 living with parents of legal custodians, pregnant women, and people securing custody of children under the age of 18), and handicap (disability)."

What this Means

Fair Housing Law really isn't that complicated. In a nutshell, it means that someone cannot discriminate against any protected class. When it comes to selling or renting a home, by law, the owner cannot discriminate against anyone based on their:

- Race or color: meaning the color of their skin or their cultural race

- National origin: meaning the country they are from

- Religion: whether they are Christian, Muslim, Buddhist, atheist or any other religion

- Sex: male or female

- Familial status: whether they have children or not

- Disability: whether they are disabled – physically or mentally

There are also other categories that are protected in many states:

- Marital status: whether the tenant-buyers are married or not

- Age: how old they are

- Sexual Orientation: heterosexual, bisexual, homosexual, asexual

That pretty much covers the protected classes. A landlord or seller could discriminate against someone based on their occupation – that isn't protected. For example, if you are an auditor for the IRS, a landlord could refuse to rent to you. However, I believe the words, "I think I'll take a look at your tax returns for the last 5 years," would be enough to get any landlord to change his mind about that. A landlord can also exclude cigarette smokers. These are not protected by Fair Housing Law.

An additional class that in some states can be protected by different law is "source of income". This particularly applies to Section 8 housing. A landlord cannot prohibit someone from renting based on the fact that they receive Section 8 housing assistance in some states. The landlord can refuse to sell their home as a rent-to-own to someone who doesn't make enough money to buy the home.

If you want to know what additional classes are protected in your state, www.Craigslist.org has most of them posted (this is not guaranteed to be complete for your area and does not cover municipalities): www.Craigslist.org/about/FHA#categories.

Some other things that are NOT protected are:

1. **Illegal activities:** If you are dealing drugs or running a illegal drug lab out of the home, the landlord can have you arrested and evict you immediately.

2. **More illegal activities**: If you are working as a prostitute or running a brothel out of the home, the landlord can have you tossed in jail and evict you.

3. **Running a business out of the home:** Even if the business you are running is legitimate, such as a day care facility, the landlord can evict you and your option fee would be forfeited if the lease agreement prohibits such activity or if the business violates local or state laws.

4. **Too many people in the home**: Most leases specify the number of people that will be living in the home (this is different than asking about whether you have children). If you let your cousin Ernie and his brood of 12 kids move in as well, you'll be violating the lease and the seller can evict you.

5. **Personal appearance**: If you are covered head to toe in tattoos and have 100 piercings on your body, the seller/landlord could refuse to sell you their rent-to-own home (most sellers would be more interested in selling

their home than in caring what you look like, so this shouldn't be too much of a problem).

Wendy's Wisdom

Fair Housing Law does not give you the right to do illegal activities or otherwise violate the terms of the contracts you signed. Its purpose is to protect you from discrimination, not allow you to illegally import stolen Mayan archeological treasures and sell them out of your garage.

Common Forms of Discrimination

Despite Fair Housing Law being pretty clear, sometimes sellers or landlords don't realize they are discriminating (or even don't care that they are). Sometimes the discrimination, especially when it's done out of the seller's ignorance, isn't that big of a deal if it doesn't affect you either way. Remember, your goal is to find a rent-to-own home, not to crucify a well-intentioned seller for a small mistake.

An example of this would be an ad that says, "Smaller home, good for single person or couple with no children." This ad violates familial and marital status and is, therefore, discriminatory. If the seller is still willing to sell or rent to you and your family, then you probably don't need to worry too much.

To be honest, if it seems clear that the person is advertising their home with obvious discriminatory exclusions in the advertisement, I don't think I would even bother calling about the house. Would you really want that person as your landlord?

Advertising Mistakes

Here are some examples of seller or rental advertisements that violate Fair Housing Law:

"Home is perfect for young couple looking for their first home"

–violates age and possibly marital status

"Wanted: a good Christian family"

– violates religion and familial status

"Mostly Hispanic neighborhood"

– violates race/color

Typically, these kinds of mistakes can happen when the owner tries to describe who the property is good for instead of giving details about the property itself.

Contact Discrimination

Discrimination can start to rear its ugly head when you try to contact the owner to get information about the property. Let's say you call an owner about a home and he tells you it's no longer available. However, a week later you still see the ad in the paper. You have a distinctive accent, as though you are from another country or the sound of your voice might give an indication as to the color of your skin. You have someone call without an accent, and the owner tells him that the home is still available. It certainly appears that the owner is discriminating against you.

You might have even called about the home and left a voicemail message and never heard back, but still see the ad running. If you have a native English speaking friend call and leave a message and get a call back, it may be that the owner is discriminating; however, they may not have received your message. It still may be a good idea to call them again.

In a situation where an owner tells you the property is no longer available or doesn't ever get back to you based on your national origin, skin color or any other protected class, you are being discriminated against.

Rental Application Discrimination

There are certain questions that a landlord should not ask on the rental application. Sometimes the question may not matter too much to you, and other times, it can impact your ability to rent the home if the owner excludes you because of your answer. Here are some rental application no-no's:

- Asking questions about a person's disability

- Asking if a (disabled) person is able to live independently

- Asking whether the applicant and co-applicant are married

- Asking you to name your children

- Requiring proof of U.S. citizenship as part of the application. This one is a bit tricky. While an owner can't discriminate based on national origin, some states now have laws that will penalize the landlord if they rent to an illegal alien. As part of documentation purposes, the owner may ask you to provide proof of citizenship, a green card or a State Department issued Visa that permits you to legally be in the United States.

Changing the Terms of the Deal or Rental Standards - To Keep You Out

Another way a seller might discriminate against you is by changing the terms of the deal or the rental qualifications. A smart seller will have a written list of rental qualifications; however, it is rare for them to do this. These qualifications should be the same no matter who applies for the home. If the seller rejects a tenant-buyer's application, he should do so only for not meeting the criteria on his written qualifications list. A seller is also supposed to give you a written notice of the rejection with an explanation of why the application was rejected. That's the way this is supposed to transpire.

However, most sellers or landlords do not create a list of written qualifications. These same sellers are also likely to accept or reject you based on their gut feeling about you, or even their personal prejudices.

If your rent-to-own application was rejected for legitimate reasons, such as your income is too low, you shouldn't be crying foul and file a discrimination complaint. The seller will easily be able to prove that they rejected you appropriately. However, if you met all of the seller's application criteria (i.e. income requirements, work history and so forth), and they rejected you because you are in a wheel chair, you have every right to claim discrimination.

Also, if the seller changes the terms to give one applicant a better deal than another, he could be in violation of Fair Housing Law. For example, let's say you are of Hispanic origin and a rent-to-own seller tells you that the terms for his house are $150,000 purchase price, $1,200 per month rent, 2% option fee and no option credits. Then the very next day he tells a white buyer that the terms are $150,000 purchase price, $1,200 per month rent, 1% option fee and $200 per month in option credits. Clearly these terms are different. This is not part of negotiations; this is simply the seller telling you his initial terms. Certainly, two different people negotiating with the same seller could reach a different agreement.

I'm only talking about the seller initially making the terms different based on who the potential buyer is.

No-Pet Policy

Sellers/landlords are entitled to have no-pet policies. However, they MUST make an exception for a handicapped person with a guide dog. Refusing to allow the guide dog because of their no-pet policy is a violation of Fair Housing Law. Additionally, if they had a no-pet policy and then made an exception for a guide dog, they cannot suddenly institute a pet deposit or monthly pet fee. Those charges did not exist before the handicapped person applied, so they cannot exist after.

Reasonable Accommodation

If you or a member of your household is disabled and you ask the seller for permission to have an entrance ramp installed, as well as modify the bathroom for access, the seller cannot deny you this right. They must allow you reasonable accommodation. However, any expense incurred for making these changes must be paid by you, not the seller.

Additionally, if you choose not to purchase the rent-to-own home, you MUST return the home to its original condition at your expense. If you are going to make modifications to the home, the seller might ask that you put a deposit into an escrow account to cover the cost of returning the home to its original condition.

What to Do If You Have Been Discriminated Against

Now that we've covered some of the ways a seller/landlord might discriminate against you, we need to look at what you can do if you feel this has happened. The Fair Housing Act is enforced by HUD, or the U.S. Department of Housing and Urban Development. If you feel you have been discriminated against, your first step is to file a complaint with HUD. They take these complaints very seriously and will do their best to protect your rights.

You can file a complaint online at www.hud.gov/offices/fheo/online-complaint.cfm. Also, at that same web address is a breakdown by state for the HUD regional office telephone numbers. By calling the appropriate telephone number, you can file your complaint by phone.

In your complaint you should tell HUD:

1. Your name and address
2. The name and address of the person you are filing the complaint against
3. The address of the property involved (if it isn't the same address as the person)
4. A short description of the incident
5. The date(s) of the incident

Once you have filed a complaint, HUD will notify you that they have received it. They will also notify the person named in the complaint that a complaint has been filed and will give that person the opportunity to submit a response. Additionally, HUD will do an investigation of the complaint to decide whether it appears the Fair Housing Act was violated.

HUD may also take quick steps, if necessary. For example, if a rent-to-own seller rejects your application by discriminating against you and then finds another buyer, HUD may step in and block the sale of the home until they have time to perform their investigation.

The first step HUD will try to take is to reach reconciliation between you and the owner of the property. This reconciliation will protect your rights as well as the public interest. If the seller fails to adhere to or refuse to honor the agreement, HUD will recommend that the Attorney General file suit against the seller.

As I said, HUD takes the Fair Housing Act very seriously and will strive to protect your rights if they have been violated. If you want to read more about HUD's process for complaints, go to: www.hud.gov/offices/fheo/complaint-process.cfm.

In the next chapter, we will look at what happens after you have found your rent-to-own home, reached a deal with the seller and they have approved your rental application. This is the step where you'll actually be moving in to your new rent-to-own home.

Chapter 16

Approved! What Do I Do Next?

Once you have been approved by your seller, you have a few little details to take care of. You know, things like moving into your new house, signing contracts and so forth.

The following is a checklist that will simplify all of the steps you need to remember. I will discuss these step by step. Note that they might not be in the exact order for your personal situation, and some items may not apply to your situation. As long as you check off each item on the list, you will stay on track.

(Note: All checklists in this book can be downloaded at www.WendyPatton.com/checklists)

Rent-to-Buy Checklist

- ☐ Create a folder for your new home
- ☐ Set up your move in date
- ☐ Draft all documents: Rental Agreement, Sales Contract, Option Agreement, Memorandum of Option, Affidavit of Liens
- ☐ Inspect the home
- ☐ Maintenance/Work to be completed

- ☐ Order pre-title work
- ☐ Check if taxes are paid
- ☐ Check if mortgage is current
- ☐ Review title work
- ☐ Get seller to complete a Lead Based Paint Disclosure and Seller's Disclosure
- ☐ Record Memorandum of Option
- ☐ Set up auto-payments, if paying mortgage payment
- ☐ Set up utilities
- ☐ Water reading (if city water)
- ☐ Water softener (if well/rental?)
- ☐ Get insurance – a Renter's Policy
- ☐ Set up credit repair for yourself (if needed)
- ☐ Sign all documents
- ☐ Additional items:

Wendy's Wisdom

www.Craigslist.org and *www.Freecycle.org* are good sources for free moving boxes.

Create a Folder for Your New Home

Once you have found your rent-to-own home, you need to start preparing for it. I strongly recommend that you get a file folder and keep all of your documents in it. This folder should have copies of all your contracts and paperwork. You should also keep copies of all payments, receipts, etc., in the folder during the lease period. An important part of being able to get a mortgage at the end of the rental period is having organized documentation to create a strong paper trail. Don't put this off, do it at the very beginning. Make a copy of every check you write to pay for rent and put it into the folder in case proof of payment will be required later.

Wendy's Wisdom

"Organizing is what you do before you do something, so that when you do it, it is not all mixed up."
– A. A. Milne, creator of Winnie-the-Pooh.

Set Up Your Move-In Date

It's almost time to move into your new rent-to-own home! Set the date with the seller. Many rent-to-own sellers will have already moved to their new home before you ever came into the picture.

If they haven't already moved out, you'll want to make sure they are out and the house is cleaned and ready for you to move in.

Draft All Documents: Rental Agreement, Sales Contract, Option Agreement, Memorandum of Option and Affidavit of Liens

Prepare the contracts before you move in so that you have everything ready to go. All of these contracts are available in my companion course, *'Rent-to-Buy'*, which is available in the "Wendy's Store" section of www.WendyPatton.com. I go into detail on this in my course with an audio step-by-step instruction CD to assist you.

Remember, as we talked about before, not all contracts are created equal. If the seller or the seller's real estate agent offers to prepare the contracts, you will be getting neutral contracts at best. At worst, you may be stuck with contracts that favor the seller instead of you. Protect yourself with good contracts.

Inspect the Home

Chapter 14 was all about home inspections. Make sure you do this. This allows you to know what you are getting into. It protects you and protects your option fee. If you do a rent-to-own without getting an inspection and then discover all kinds of problems while you are living there, you might be on the hook for some of the repairs (depending on your contracts). If you choose not to buy, you would forfeit the option fee.

After you get the home inspected, renegotiate with the seller or have them perform some repairs, if needed.

Maintenance/Work to be Completed

If there are issues from the home inspection, and as part of your agreement with the seller they need to be resolved before you move in, you'll want to check to make sure the seller is on top of them. Typically, it is better to have issues resolved *before* you move in. It's less hassle for you because you don't have to make arrangements to meet the repair person when you are supposed to be at work. Also, by having the issues taken care of before you move in, it helps ensure that the seller gets them done instead of putting them off.

Order Pre-Title Work

This is a part of the "qualifying the seller" process that we talked about in Chapter 13. You'll need help with this; start with either your real estate agent or your real estate attorney. If you aren't working with either, you can try contacting a title company or an attorney, depending on your state. Receiving the pre-title work can take a few days or more so you'll want to get this ordered as soon as the seller approves your rental application.

Check if Taxes Have Been Paid

You'll want to make sure the seller is paying their property taxes and that they are current. If the seller has a mortgage, there is a good chance that the lender requires an escrow account to cover property taxes and insurance. In this case, you'll probably be able to verify that the taxes are current when you verify that the mortgage is current. However, not all mortgage lenders require an escrow account, and some sellers don't have mortgages. In this case, you'll need to verify from another source. Usually, you can check with your local Tax Assessor's office (or whatever it is called where you live) to make sure the taxes are current. Many assessors' offices now allow you to do this online. Otherwise, you should call the office.

If the seller's taxes aren't current or haven't been paid when you are ready to buy the home, the seller won't be able to sell the home until the taxes are paid in full. If the seller has enough equity, the taxes would be paid out of the proceeds from the sale. However, if the seller doesn't have enough equity, the seller would have to pay the taxes themselves before the home could be sold.

Check if the Mortgage is Current

The best way to do this is to get the seller to sign the Authorization to Release in Chapter 13. If the seller won't sign, you'll want to require them to provide you with proof that their mortgage is current. To do this, the seller could obtain a letter from their lender verifying that the payments are current and that there are no past due amounts owed.

Wendy's Wisdom

These steps are about protecting your interests as a buyer. You'll want to make sure that when the time comes to buy, the seller is able to sell you their home.

Review Title Work

Once the pre-title work is complete, it's time to review it for issues. I definitely recommend asking for help with this step. Your real estate agent, your real estate attorney or the title agent can assist you. Ask them for help. Make sure they explain things to you so that you understand how to deal with any problems or issues.

The seller won't be able to sell you their home if there are any problems with the title. By checking now, it gives the seller time to resolve potential issues, or it gives you time to find another rent-to-own home if the seller is not able to sell.

Get Seller to Complete a Lead Based Paint Disclosure and Seller's Disclosure

It's a good idea to have these forms completed in advance. Many buyers like to review them before they even make an offer on the home in case they need to factor information from these forms into their offer.

Once you have reviewed the forms, you will need to sign off on them. This means that you have seen them and acknowledged the information on these forms.

Record Memorandum of Option

Once you have completed all of the paperwork and signed them along with the seller, you'll want to take the Memorandum of Option and record it at your Registrar of Deeds, County Recorder's Office or the government entity in your area that handles recorded documents. Remember, the Memorandum must be notarized for it to be recorded.

Set Up Auto-Payments, If Paying Mortgage Payment

If you will be paying the seller's mortgage payment directly, it's a good idea to set up automatic payments so you won't have to worry about missing payments. This also gives the seller some peace of mind knowing that their mortgage payment is being paid. Both you and the seller have a vested interest in making certain that these mortgage payments are made.

If you miss just one payment, it could invalidate your option and you could lose your option fee along with the right to buy the home.

Set Up Utilities

You will need to get the utilities transferred to your name. You'll need to call in advance and schedule the transfer for the move in date. You want to make sure this is done so that you don't run into any issues with meeting your obligations on the Option Agreement or the Lease Agreement.

You'll need to do this in advance to give the utility companies a chance to schedule a final meter reading before you move in.

If you work out an agreement with the seller to move in early, you'll want to schedule the utility transfer for the day you move in. If a seller is generous enough to let you move in a few days early, make sure the utilities are transferred on time to pay them back for their generosity.

Water Reading (If City Water)

If your rent-to-own is on city water, the seller may not want the account transferred to your name. In most municipalities, unpaid water bills, unlike other utilities, can create a lien against the property. Therefore, the seller may want to continue paying the water bills and invoice you each month. Although the account will not be transferred, you should still request a meter reading for your move-in date. You will be responsible for reimbursing the seller for water used from that date forward.

Water Softener (if Well – Rental?)

If the home isn't on city water but is on a well, you will most likely have a water softener in the home. In some homes the softener is owned, and in some homes the softener is rented. If the softener is rented, you'll probably need to transfer the rental contract to your name. This allows you to receive the bills directly and make sure they are paid.

In general, any bills that you are responsible for paying should be sent to you directly so you can pay them directly and on time.

Get Insurance – a Renter's Policy

The owner of the home is still responsible for providing homeowner's insurance to protect the home itself, however, his policy will be a "dwelling-only" policy, meaning that only the structure is covered, not its contents. Your valuables are not covered under the seller's insurance and you will need to get a renter's insurance policy to protect your possessions. I strongly recommend you do this. There are only a few things worse than losing everything you own and not being able to replace any of it for lack of insurance. A Renter's Policy is a must!

Set up Credit Repair for Yourself (if needed)

This is one of the most important steps you should take. If your credit needs improvement before you can qualify for a mortgage, you absolutely want to jump right on this. You should sign up for this as soon as you are approved by the seller and have scheduled your move in date. If you are working with a seller who has read my book *'Rent-to-Sell'*, they will almost certainly require you to take this step.

Without this, you may not be able to qualify for a mortgage when it comes time to buy. A credit repair company will help you get your credit in shape so that you can qualify for a mortgage. If you are looking for a quality credit repair company, go to: *www.RenttoOwnCreditRepair.com.* Don't put your option fee at risk and don't waste all of those months of rental payments with nothing to show for it. I will go into details about credit repair in Chapter 17.

Sign All Documents

It's time to meet with the seller and sign all of the documents. Typically, you would do this before you move in. This allows you to lock in the deal and prevents the seller from finding another buyer. You would pay the option fee to the seller at the time all documents are signed. You might pay the rent and security deposit to the seller at this time as well or when you take possession of the home. Bring a pen or two!

Checklist During Tenancy

While you are renting the home, there is also a checklist you can follow that will help you stay on track to make sure you are able to buy the home at the end of the rental period.

☐ Meet with a mortgage broker and set up a plan
☐ Get into credit repair
☐ Always pay with a personal check or cashier's check that comes from your bank account each month

- ☐ Keep a copy of each month's payment in your home folder
- ☐ Pay monthly rent payments on time and in full
- ☐ Pay all bills on time to clean up credit
- ☐ Continue to follow up with mortgage broker on credit status

Congratulations! Now that you have moved into your new rent-to-own home, you can start getting on track for the dream of homeownership. Follow the steps you need to improve your credit. Make sure you adhere to the terms of the Lease and Option Agreement so that you can follow through.

In the next chapter, we will cover how to ensure that everyone is getting paid - making sure that the bank receives the mortgage payment, property taxes are paid, you are paying the rent, and so forth.

Part 5:

What to do During the Rent-to-Own Term And How to Close the Deal

Chapter 17

Repairing/Improving Credit –

Paying Bills on Time & Paying Down Debts

The recent credit crunch has made qualifying for financing significantly more difficult for even those with good credit. It used to be that many rent-to-own tenant-buyers could just make on-time payments for a while and then they would be able to get a mortgage. Times have changed. All of those high-risk mortgages to people with less than perfect credit are gone.

Making your mortgage payments on time is important, but it is not enough for foreclosure-weary lenders. They want to see improved credit scores. This is why credit repair is more important than ever. As a tenant-buyer, you should be <u>serious</u> about getting your credit into shape. There is absolutely no reason to be a tenant-buyer if you aren't. You might as well just live in a rental. If you aren't serious about improving your credit, you'll just be throwing away your option fee.

Wendy's Wisdom

Credit repair is absolutely critical. Unless you already have excellent credit, this is a chapter you definitely need to focus on. You won't be able to get a mortgage if you don't improve your credit.

Working with a Mortgage Broker

The first important step for you to take toward qualifying for a mortgage is to stay in touch with your mortgage broker. A good mortgage broker can give you an overall guideline for steps you need to take to get your credit in shape so that you are mortgage-ready and can become a homeowner.

Mortgage brokers are wired in to the changing requirements of qualifying for a mortgage (and requirements are changing frequently). They will be able to help guide you through the process. Not all mortgage brokers are credit experts; some just know how to write loans. They may be able to tell you what your current credit score is and what bad marks you have and that's about it.

If you are looking for a mortgage broker who can do more than just write loans, go to the "Rent-to-Own" section of my website, and click on the "Rent-to-Own" link at the top. Then simply click on the "Mortgage Lender" box at the right for a list of lenders who do national lending and know credit repair and lease options.

Credit Reports

It is very important to be aware of what is on your credit report and work to fix the bad marks. There are a number of factors that can cause poor credit, such as late payments, foreclosures, bankruptcy, settled debts, unpaid debts, over-extended credit and lack of credit history.

You will want to focus your efforts on maximizing your credit score during the rental period. Being perfect may not be necessary. Your lender will tell you what you need to focus on. Let's take a look at some things you can do to improve your credit.

Paying on Time

This is a critical step. You MUST make your payments on time. Not just your monthly rent, but also all of your other bills. Every bill that is a paid late s a ding against your credit score. Even one ding after you start renting may cause a lender to reject your loan application. Just as late payments are damaging to credit scores, on time payments can help boost credit scores.

Stop Using Credit Cards

Tenant-buyers with a lot of debt or over-extended credit need to stop using their credit cards and stop accumulating debt. If you are serious about buying a home, you need to stop accumulating other debts. You don't want to buy a new car, buy furniture on a payment plan, etc., - *nothing*. You need to focus on paying bills on time and paying off all debts.

The more debts you have, the lower your credit score and the lower the amount of mortgage you can qualify for – if you can qualify at all.

Building New Credit

This applies only if you don't have enough established credit accounts to qualify for a mortgage. It should NOT be used if you already have established credit that is in bad shape.

In the case of tenant-buyers who have very little credit history and need to build their credit, it can be useful to establish a couple of new credit accounts. For example, you may get a new credit card or purchase furniture with financing. I know I just said you shouldn't do this, but I'll explain.

With either type of financing (credit card or purchasing furniture or appliances with financing), you should make monthly payments to help establish a credit history. However, you should definitely PAY OFF these accounts IN FULL at least 3 months before it comes time to apply for a mortgage. Otherwise, the debts on these credit accounts may hurt your chances of getting a mortgage. A mortgage lender should help you with this plan. Remember, this is only for tenant-buyers who don't have enough credit, NOT for tenant-buyers who are trying to rebuild their credit.

Do-It-Yourself Credit Repair

Challenging Items on a Credit Report

Another important step toward improving credit is to challenge any items that appear on your credit report that are invalid. In cases of credit fraud or even errors, sometimes an account appears on a credit report that doesn't belong to you. These accounts should be challenged to get them removed.

I'll talk later in this chapter about using credit repair companies that can handle this for you.

Closing Old Accounts

Tenant-buyers with long established credit histories may have numerous old accounts that are no longer used. For example, if you purchased furniture with financing through a credit company, that credit company would set up an account. The account is not automatically closed when you pay the debt off. Surprisingly, it doesn't even get automatically closed if the furniture store goes out of business. However, when lenders consider how much they can loan you, they do take the available credit for that account into consideration - whether you are using it or not.

It may be a good idea to close out some of these accounts, however, talk to your mortgage lender first. Sometimes closing an account can make a credit score drop. Old established accounts with no outstanding balance can help a credit score go up. So you'll need to balance the advantages of having paid off accounts versus the disadvantage of having too much available credit. You would want to do this early on instead of waiting until you are close to applying for a mortgage. Strangely, if the accounts are closed when you are applying for financing, it won't help you.

Paying Off Other Debts

Many buyers are denied mortgages because they have too much other debt. Even if they can get a mortgage, the amount they can qualify for will be reduced because of the other debts.

You will want to strike a balance between paying off other debts and saving for a down payment. When it comes to paying off debts, an excellent technique is to focus on the smallest debt first and then work progressively upwards.

For example, let's say you have the following debts:

Debt Type	Debt Amount	Monthly Payment
Gas Credit Card	$325	$24
Retail/ Merchant Credit Card	$615	$40
Visa	$2,200	$70
Auto	$17,500	$395

We'll also say that you have an extra $175 per month in income after all bills are paid, groceries bought and so forth. Some people may make the mistake of dividing that $175 between all of the debts, such as an extra $15 towards the gas credit card, $20 towards the retail credit card, $30 towards the Visa® and $110 towards the car payment.

In fact, this way will take forever to pay off the debts.

Others may pay the extra towards the highest interest rate debt first. This is a smart idea, but when it comes to qualifying for a mortgage there is a much better way to pay off debts: Focus on the smallest debt first and then work your way up.

In this case, the smallest debt is the gas credit card for $325. Combining the regular monthly payment of $24 with the additional $175 in extra money you have that month, makes for a total payment of $199. If you make the $199 payment in the first month on the gas card (and pay the minimum on all of the other balances ON-TIME), the next month's balance will be approximately $130 (because there will be some interest charged). In the second month, you can pay off the first debt with a payment of $130 and still have $69 left over from the $199 total.

That $69 should be applied with the $40 payment on the retail/merchant credit card for a total payment of $109 in the second month. In the third month, you have now paid off the gas credit card and can make a total payment of $239 towards the retail credit card, which now has a balance of $515. How did the payment go up to $239, you ask?

By paying off the smallest debt balance first, you can now roll that monthly payment of $24 onto paying the next debt, so the total payment of $24 from the gas card, plus $40 from the retail credit card, plus $175 in extra funds equals a total of $239.

At this rate, you will be able to pay off the retail credit card in just over two more months. After that, you will be able to make a total payment of $309 per month against the Visa® card debt. It will take about 7 months to pay off the Visa® card at this rate. In about 1 year, you will have paid off the gas credit card, the retail credit card and the Visa® card.

Wendy's Wisdom

This technique is a great way to get your debts under control and improve your credit. As you read on, you'll see how paying off these small debts can greatly increase the amount of mortgage you can qualify for.

Not only does paying off these debts help your credit, but it also has two other benefits. Paying more than the minimum amount on these debts can also improve your credit score, but more importantly, you have freed up $134 in monthly expenses ($24 from the gas card, $40 from the retail card and $70 from the Visa® card).

Eliminating these monthly payments can substantially increase the amount of mortgage you can qualify for.

For example, eliminating the $24 payment for the gas card can increase the mortgage amount by approximately $4,000. Eliminate the retail credit card debt payment, and the mortgage can increase by another $7,000. These amounts will depend, of course, on the interest rate of the mortgage and your monthly income, among other things. This should give you an idea of how a small monthly payment can make a big difference on the amount financed. This is why taking on new debt is very dangerous. Just as eliminating a small monthly payment can increase the amount of mortgage you can qualify for, adding a small monthly payment can greatly reduce the amount of mortgage you can qualify for.

Let's say you reach a deal on a rent-to-own home with a seller for $150,000 and your loan officer tells you that's all the mortgage you can qualify for once you've improved your credit. You take all the appropriate steps to improve your credit during the rental period, but then you decide you really want a new dining room set because that plastic patio table really doesn't cut it inside your new home. You find a great sale with 0% interest financing and your monthly payment will only be $24. That's a great sale, right? Except there is one major problem. That $24 monthly payment just reduced the amount of mortgage you can qualify for by $4,000, which means you can only get a mortgage of $146,000 instead of $150,000. Now you won't be able to buy your rent-to-own home and you may lose your option fee, plus any option credits you've accumulated as well, unless your seller will work with you.

Wendy's Wisdom

Don't incur new debts during your rental period. This is a time to be repairing your credit, not adding to your debts. The only tenant-buyers who should be taking on new debts are those who are trying to establish credit (see above,) and they should pay those debts off IN FULL at least 3 months before the end of the rental period.

Building Up a Down Payment

In addition to improving credit, you may also need to save up for a larger down payment. How much of a down payment you will need depends on the type of financing your mortgage broker can get you.

One issue to be aware of is that as the credit crunch continues, lenders may restrict financing even further. This is another reason why it is good for you to stay in touch with your mortgage broker to know how lender's rules are changing and what you will need when it comes time to purchase your home.

There are still many FHA programs that might work for you that have a minimal amount down. It will definitely be a benefit for you to have MORE of a down payment than less. You can accumulate a down payment several ways. The option fee you paid at the beginning will be a part of your down payment. You can also accumulate option credits if you negotiated them with the seller, and you can save additional money on your own as well.

In our previous example of paying off debts, we had you paying off the gas credit card, the retail credit card and the Visa® card. In fact, it might be better for you to only pay off the gas credit card and retail credit card, for example, and continue making normal payments on the Visa® card and save the extra money for the down payment.

On a 24-month rent-to-own option, it took the first 5 months to pay off the two smaller accounts. After that, you would be able to save $239 per month for 19 months, or a total of another $4,541.

This accumulated down payment might be more beneficial than paying off the Visa® card.

Wendy's Wisdom

Another great way to save towards your down payment is income tax returns. Do you get a check back from the government? Save it! During a 2 year option period, this could be the accumulation of 2 years of saved tax returns.

Your individual plan you should be developed with your mortgage lender. As I already said, however, many lenders do not understand or know how to work with a rent-to-own buyer. To find a good lender, go to www.WendyPatton.com and go to the "Rent-to-Own" section for information on a mortgage lender in your area.

Have a Professional Assist You

Credit Repair

There are also credit repair companies that will help you with credit repair. They specialize in repair and some will guarantee results. Most of the time, credit repair companies are necessary to help you rebuild your credit. They know the laws and loopholes that will get some, if not all, derogatory information off of someone's credit. I have seen them remove bankruptcies, foreclosures, collection accounts, etc. from a person's credit report. You can check out: www.RentToOwnCreditRepair.com to get more information.

Wendy's Wisdom

Some rent-to-own sellers may require you to get into credit repair, if you have credit issues, as part of the option agreement. If you are trying to rebuild your credit, I definitely recommend using a reputable credit repair company to help you.

If you take the necessary steps, you should be able to qualify for a mortgage and purchase your new rent-to-own home. Sometimes things don't always work out as planned - you might need more time or some other problem crops up. In the next chapter, we look at how to handle problems that might occur when buying your home as a rent-to-own.

Chapter 18

Oops, Not Everything Went According to Plan

Even the best laid plans and the best intentions sometimes go awry. Circumstances outside of our control often occur. Sometimes peoples' intentions aren't the best and you may need to take action.

This chapter isn't intended to scare you, it's meant to help you be ready in case something doesn't go as planned. Hopefully, you won't need anything in this chapter. However, in some cases you might, and that is when you can use the following information to help guide you.

Extensions

In some cases, you want to buy the seller's home but your credit score hasn't improved enough, you've been foreclosed on or have declared bankruptcy too recently before you found your rent-to-own home and you can't yet qualify for a mortgage. If this is the case, you would want to extend the lease period. It's completely up to the seller whether or not to grant the extension. They aren't obligated to do anything but adhere to the terms of the original agreement. In most cases, though, they will want to grant that extension. If the seller is reluctant to extend, you can point out the following:

- If they put their home back on the market, it could sit empty for months before they find a new buyer or new tenant-buyer and it could cost them thousands of dollars. You want to buy; you just need more time.

- If they find a new tenant-buyer, they will have to start all over again and it will take at least as long to sell their home, if not longer.

- There is no guarantee that a new tenant-buyer would want (or be qualified) to buy at the end of the rental period. You do want to buy now.

- They may have to sell for a significantly *lower* price if they try to sell to a conventional buyer.

All of these factors spell out that the seller really should consider working with you on extending the rental period. That being said, however, the seller may ask for a concession in return. This is fairly reasonable, since you are asking them for a large concession of more time. Here are several options the seller might ask for:

Increasing the Sale Price – If the housing market has appreciated where you live, the seller may ask for some of that appreciation in the form of an increased sale price. If the housing market has depreciated, this request won't work. Even if you were willing to grant the increased price, your mortgage lender will order an appraisal on the home when you apply for the loan. If the appraisal isn't high enough, the lender won't give you the mortgage amount you qualify for. If the seller asks for more money even though the home is worth less, you won't be able to get a mortgage.

Increasing the Option Fee – The seller might ask you for additional option money. This gives them more security that you are going to follow through with the purchase. The more money you have paid in option fees, the less likely you are to walk away from it.

Of course, this money should apply against the purchase price when you buy. Make sure you have this in writing. If you are really serious about buying the home but just need more time, this would be a good concession to give to the seller because all of the money you put down as an option fee counts against your purchase price.

Increasing the Rent – A seller could ask you for additional rent money. This can be the case, particularly if your monthly rental payments aren't enough to cover their mortgage payment. This would help ease the monthly strain for them when they have to cover the difference.

Decreasing Option Credits – If the seller agreed to give you option credits during the initial lease period, they might want to take some of them away during the extension. This effectively amounts to more money to the seller when you buy their home without the seller having to increase the purchase price. Obviously, this isn't very desirable for you. It could also be problematic if you need a certain amount of money for a down payment to get approved for the mortgage, and losing some of your option credits toward the down payment drops you below that amount.

One potential issue a seller may encounter when granting an extension is the capital gains tax issue. If the seller stands to make a moderate to large profit on the sale of their home they may be liable to pay tax on that profit when they sell if they extend beyond the capital gains exclusion period. But, this is not your problem as a buyer. This is something to be aware of because it may cause a seller might object to an extension.

If you and the seller agree to an extension, the details should be put into writing and signed by both of you. This prevents misunderstandings and gives you legal protection. Make sure you itemize all changes, including how long the extension is valid. Additionally, if the extension paperwork is more than one page, both you and the seller should initial every page. Usually it will be just a few sentences to explain what changed or what you are agreeing to. Just make sure it is in writing for all parties to be protected.

Buying with Changes

In some cases, you are able to buy at the end of the initial option period, but either need or want to renegotiate certain points of the sale.

For example, if the appraisal from the lender comes in too low for the home, you might request that the seller decrease the purchase price accordingly, otherwise you won't be able to buy the home. This might happen in cases where a housing market has continued to depreciate during the lease period. Understand that the seller is not obligated to change the price. Given that the home has appraised for less, however, the seller won't be able to sell it to someone else for more. Point that out to the seller. Also point out that you are ready to buy now, and if they try to sell to someone else, their home may sit empty for months. They'll still have to sell it for the appraised price so it will end up costing them even more.

Another change that might come up is that the closing costs from the lender may be higher than you originally anticipated. You might need to request a *seller concession* to help cover those closing costs. Typically, this is added on top of the purchase price so it doesn't cost the seller anything, but it can only be added to the purchase price if the home appraises for enough.

There might also be condition issues with the home that you weren't initially aware of, but learned about while living there during the rental period. If these issues weren't disclosed on the seller's disclosure, it's not unreasonable to ask that the seller cover the cost of those issues or decrease the purchase price accordingly.

Choosing Not to Exercise the Option

Sometimes you simply decide that you don't want to buy the home. Either you decided that the seller's home wasn't right for you or becoming a homeowner wasn't right for you. Whatever the circumstances, you have decided to move on.

If this is the case and you have used my contracts, you need to notify the seller in writing before the rental period expires. In most cases, you need to give thirty days notice to move out. This gives the seller time to prepare to put their home back on the market. You have to fulfill your rental agreement.

There are some things you'll need to keep in mind:

- Option Fee – The option fee is <u>non-refundable</u>. As long as the seller lived up to their obligations in the contracts, it belongs to them.

- Option Credits - Any option credits you accumulated would also be forfeited. They only apply if you buy the home.

- Condition of the home – You must return the home to the seller in the same condition it was in when you moved in, less normal wear and tear. If there are damages to the home, it is your obligation to fix them or be financially responsible for them. Any security deposit you paid to the seller would apply against damages. You will need to provide the seller with a new mailing address to send any remainder of the security deposit to you. If the damages exceed the security deposit, the seller can sue you for the balance. I am sure you would leave the home in good condition, but if not, expect to pay for any damages.

Evictions

If you stop paying the rent or break another rule of the rental agreement, the seller may evict you. Typically, the main reason you would be evicted is if you stop paying the rent, but you can also be evicted for violating other terms of the lease, such as selling drugs out of the home.

Needless to say, if you are evicted, your right to purchase the home, your option fee, any improvements you have made to the property, as well as any option credits would all be forfeited. Don't let this happen to you! If something happens in your life, such as losing your job and you can no longer afford to pay the rent, TELL THE SELLER. You will be much better off directly talking with the seller and trying to work out a solution. Certainly, if you can't afford to pay the rent, you won't be able to keep living in the home. You will be much better off if the seller releases you from the lease than if they have to evict you. If you get evicted, you are going to have a hard time finding a new place to live because most landlords won't rent to tenants who have been evicted. This would be another huge snag on your credit report.

Want to Buy, But the Seller Can't or Won't Sell

This is your worst-case scenario. You've paid your monthly rent on time every month, you followed all of the terms of the lease, you worked to improve your credit and qualified for a mortgage; but when it comes time to buy, the seller can't or won't sell to you.

Before we look at how to handle this type of situation, let's look at why something like this might happen. Here are some reasons the seller might not be able to sell to you:

- They have a *cloud* on their title preventing them from selling

- They owe more on the home than your purchase price and don't have the money to make up the difference

In most cases, these problems are easily preventable. I talked about them earlier in the book. If the seller has a cloud on their title, you should have seen it in the pre-title work that you pulled as part of your "screening the seller" process. If they owe more than the home is selling for, you would have seen it when you got their mortgage information as part of the "screening the seller" process. However, sometimes the cloud appears on the title after you do the title work, or the seller might refinance the home to pull money out after you have moved in. By the way, if you recorded the *Memorandum of Option* using my contracts, it would block the seller from being able to refinance while you are renting.

On the other side of things, there are situations that might come up where the seller *won't* sell to you. This is almost always about money. The typical situation would be that the home has appreciated significantly in value during your rental period and the seller doesn't want to sell it for the original price. They want to sell it for a higher price. In a rare situation, the seller might be unwilling to sell because they want to move back into the home or they want to sell it to someone else.

Okay, so how do you handle situations where the seller won't or can't sell? If you used my contracts, you have strong measures of protection in place to help you. I already talked about prevention by doing the proper seller screening and recording the *Memorandum of Option*. Assuming you have done those things, the situations where the seller wouldn't or couldn't sell would be pretty rare. But should it come up, your next step is to get legal help. This is definitely a case where you don't want to try to work it out on your own. I've talked about Pre-Paid Legal before, but if you don't have it, you would definitely want to sign up for it if you found yourself in this situation. You can learn more about Pre-Paid Legal at www.GotLegalPlans.com. Just sign up, and help is a phone call away.

In the case where the seller won't sell, you would sue them for *specific performance*. You are suing them to force them to sell you their home. They signed contracts. You fulfilled your obligations, so they need to fulfill theirs. If you used the correct contracts, you shouldn't have too much difficulty enforcing them and getting the seller to sell you the home.

**Remember your Goal:
To BUY Your New Home!**

If you are in a situation where the seller can't sell, resolution would depend on why they cannot sell. If it is because of a clouded title, it may simply take a little extra time to have the cloud removed. This might be more complicated in some cases than in others.

What do you do if the cloud can't be removed or if the seller owes more than your purchase price and can't make up the difference? While this type of situation is very rare, I would be remiss in saying that it can't happen. Your options in this type of situation are:

1. Wait until it gets resolved

2. Ask for a refund to get out

3. Final option; call an attorney

These types of problems don't come up very often, so I don't want you to worry. Remember, this chapter has been about preparing you on how to handle them if they do come up. If you follow the rest of the book and use the right contracts, you are unlikely to run into problems. Keep that in mind and don't let the potential possibility of problems keep you from the dream of homeownership.

In the next chapter, we'll talk about the closing, when you are finally buying your rent-to-own home.

Chapter 19

Completing the Transaction and

Buying the Home

You've made it! It's time to buy your rent-to-own home. Congratulations!

Before you purchase your home, you are going to need homeowner's insurance. The homeowner's policy will cover both the dwelling and the contents. This is different than from renter's insurance policy which only covered your possessions. Insurance rates can vary greatly between companies and from one part of a city to another. Because of this, you'll want to shop around.

Most mortgage lenders are going to want to escrow your property taxes and insurance costs. This means that you will be paying a monthly payment into the escrow account, and when the tax and insurance bills come due, the escrow account will pay for them out of the payments you've been making. This is a measure of protection for the lender to ensure that the taxes and insurance are getting paid. Additionally, many lenders are going to want the first year of insurance paid in advance before you can close on the home; so when you start paying into the escrow account, you are prepaying the next year's payment. You will definitely want to check with your mortgage lender about their requirements for homeowner's insurance so that you are prepared at closing time.

The HUD-1

When it comes time to close, there are some things that are helpful to know, particularly with the HUD-1 settlement statement. The HUD-1 statement contains all of the numbers for your closing and will show how much money you will be paying, the amount of the mortgage, all of your credits and so forth. Fortunately this isn't too complicated, because you can always ask questions and ask for help from your closing agent, real estate agent or attorney.

The HUD-1 settlement statement details where all of the money is going. The HUD-1 (or HUD as it is commonly called) is mandatory everywhere in the country as required in Section 4 of RESPA (Real Estate Settlement and Procedures Act). The HUD is very important to you. It covers all of the financial details of the purchase of your home, ranging from the purchase price to crediting your option fee and option credits. The HUD is truly the nuts and bolts of the closing and purchase of your home.

According to RESPA, you are supposed to be given a copy of the HUD at least one day prior to your closing. Unfortunately, this doesn't always happen if the title company or attorney gets stuck waiting for paperwork from other sources.

Here is the thing about the HUD: mistakes can happen. It's very important for you to review the HUD (preferably with your real estate agent or attorney) to make sure it's accurate. Rent-to-own home sales are a bit more complex and unusual compared to the average real estate transaction so the closing agent that prepares the HUD may miss something. Check everything that you can. Confirm the purchase price, your option fee, any option credits the seller gave you and any other provisions in your agreement. Make sure they are all reflected accurately.

The following is a blank copy of the HUD-1 settlement statement for you to reference as I will discuss some sections in this chapter that are important to you.

A. **Settlement Statement**

U.S. Department of Housing
and Urban Development

OMB Approval No. 2502-0265
(expires 11/30/2009)

B. Type of Loan

1. ☐ FHA 2. ☐ FmHA 3. ☐ Conv. Unins.	6. File Number:	7. Loan Number:
4. ☐ VA 5. ☐ Conv. Ins.		8. Mortgage Insurance Case Number:

C. Note: This form is furnished to give you a statement of actual settlement costs. Amounts paid to and by the settlement agent are shown. Items marked "(p.o.c.)" were paid outside the closing; they are shown here for informational purposes and are not included in the totals.

D. Name & Address of Borrower:	E. Name & Address of Seller:	F. Name & Address of Lender:
		d

G. Property Location:	H. Settlement Agent:	
	Place of Settlement:	I. Settlement Date:

J. Summary of Borrower's Transaction		**K. Summary of Seller's Transaction**	
100. Gross Amount Due From Borrower		**400. Gross Amount Due To Seller**	
101. Contract sales price		401. Contract sales price	
102. Personal property		402. Personal property	
103. Settlement charges to borrower (line 1400)		403.	
104.		404.	
105.		405.	
Adjustments for items paid by seller in advance		**Adjustments for items paid by seller in advance**	
106. City/town taxes to		406. City/town taxes to	
107. County taxes to		407. County taxes to	
108. Assessments to		408. Assessments to	
109.		409.	
110.		410.	
111.		411.	
112.		412.	
120. Gross Amount Due From Borrower		**420. Gross Amount Due To Seller**	
200. Amounts Paid By Or In Behalf Of Borrower		**500. Reductions In Amount Due To Seller**	
201. Deposit or earnest money		501. Excess deposit (see instructions)	
202. Principal amount of new loan(s)		502. Settlement charges to seller (line 1400)	
203. Existing loan(s) taken subject to		503. Existing loan(s) taken subject to	
204.		504. Payoff of first mortgage loan	
205.		505. Payoff of second mortgage loan	
206.		506.	
207.		507.	
208.		508.	
209.		509.	
Adjustments for items unpaid by seller		**Adjustments for items unpaid by seller**	
210. City/town taxes to		510. City/town taxes to	
211. County taxes to		511. County taxes to	
212. Assessments to		512. Assessments to	
213.		513.	
214.		514.	
215.		515.	
216.		516.	
217.		517.	
218.		518.	
219.		519.	
220. Total Paid By/For Borrower		**520. Total Reduction Amount Due Seller**	
300. Cash At Settlement From/To Borrower		**600. Cash At Settlement To/From Seller**	
301. Gross amount due from borrower (line 120)		601. Gross amount due to seller (line 420)	
302. Less amounts paid by/for borrower (line 220)	( )	602. Less reductions in amt. due seller (line 520)	( )
303. Cash ☐ From ☐ To Borrower		**603. Cash** ☐ To ☐ From Seller	0.00

Section 5 of the Real Estate Settlement Procedures Act (RESPA) requires the following: • HUD must develop a Special Information Booklet to help persons borrowing money to finance the purchase of residential real estate to better understand the nature and costs of real estate settlement services; • Each lender must provide the booklet to all applicants from whom it receives or for whom it prepares a written application to borrow money to finance the purchase of residential real estate; • Lenders must prepare and distribute with the Booklet a Good Faith Estimate of the settlement costs that the borrower is likely to incur in connection with the settlement. These disclosures are mandatory.

Section 4(a) of RESPA mandates that HUD develop and prescribe this standard form to be used at the time of loan settlement to provide full disclosure of all charges imposed upon the borrower and seller. These are third party disclosures that are designed to provide the borrower with pertinent information during the settlement process in order to be a better shopper.

The Public Reporting Burden for this collection of information is estimated to average one hour per response, including the time for reviewing instructions, searching existing data sources, gathering and maintaining the data needed, and completing and reviewing the collection of information.

This agency may not collect this information, and you are not required to complete this form, unless it displays a currently valid OMB control number.

The information requested does not lend itself to confidentiality.

L. Settlement Charges

	Paid From Borrowers Funds at Settlement	Paid From Seller's Funds at Settlement
700. Total Sales/Broker's Commission based on price $ @ % =		
Division of Commission (line 700) as follows:		
701. $ to		
702. $ to		
703. Commission paid at Settlement		
704.		
800. Items Payable In Connection With Loan		
801. Loan Origination Fee %		
802. Loan Discount %		
803. Appraisal Fee to		
804. Credit Report to		
805. Lender's Inspection Fee		
806. Mortgage Insurance Application Fee to		
807. Assumption Fee		
808.		
809.		
810.		
811.		
900. Items Required By Lender To Be Paid In Advance		
901. Interest from to @$ /day		
902. Mortgage Insurance Premium for months to		
903. Hazard Insurance Premium for years to		
904. years to		
905.		
1000. Reserves Deposited With Lender		
1001. Hazard insurance months@$ per month		
1002. Mortgage insurance months@$ per month		
1003. City property taxes months@$ per month		
1004. County property taxes months@$ per month		
1005. Annual assessments months@$ per month		
1006. months@$ per month		
1007. months@$ per month		
1008. months@$ per month		
1100. Title Charges		
1101. Settlement or closing fee to		
1102. Abstract or title search to		
1103. Title examination to		
1104. Title insurance binder to		
1105. Document preparation to		
1106. Notary fees to		
1107. Attorney's fees to		
(includes above items numbers:)		
1108. Title insurance to		
(includes above items numbers:)		
1109. Lender's coverage $		
1110. Owner's coverage $		
1111.		
1112.		
1113.		
1200. Government Recording and Transfer Charges		
1201. Recording fees: Deed $; Mortgage $; Releases $		
1202. City/county tax/stamps: Deed $; Mortgage $		
1203. State tax/stamps: Deed $; Mortgage $		
1204.		
1205.		
1300. Additional Settlement Charges		
1301. Survey to		
1302. Pest inspection to		
1303.		
1304.		
1305.		
1400. Total Settlement Charges (enter on lines 103, Section J and 502, Section K)		

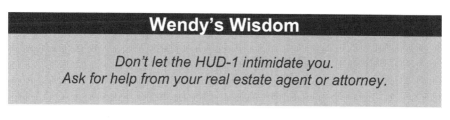

Wendy's Wisdom

Don't let the HUD-1 intimidate you.
Ask for help from your real estate agent or attorney.

HUD-1 Review

As I've said, the HUD-1 is the nuts and bolts of the closing. It covers all of the numbers. Those numbers are very important to you, which is why you want to check it carefully. You don't have to be an expert to catch mistakes. Here are some key areas to look for in the HUD (these numbers correspond to the section numbers that appear on the HUD):

- *Lines 101 & 401 – Contract Sales Price.* These should match each other and should be the amount shown on your Sales Contract with the seller.

- *Lines 106, 107 & 406, 407 – Property Taxes on the City and County level.* Taxes are prorated based on what you agree with the seller in the Purchase Agreement. Title offices are accustomed to standard purchase agreements. If you negotiate something different, it may be overlooked. In most states, property taxes are paid in arrears; therefore, you would need to pay the taxes after the date of closing. The taxes would be pro-rated from the closing date to the "taxes due" date to determine your portion and the seller's portion. Conversely, in most of Michigan, taxes are paid in advance, therefore, the seller would be credited the pro-rated taxes back based on the HUD.

- Lines 200, 201, 202 – *Amounts Paid by Borrower.* These numbers should reflect any down payments you have made, including your Option Fee, the amount of the mortgage (principal only – if you are financing closing costs they'll be elsewhere). If you have Option Credits, you should make sure they appear in this section. They may be either in 201 or they may add them in on 204 or another blank line in this section.

There are also some other sections of the HUD where you'll see numbers. I won't go into every detail, but I want you to have a general understanding.

- Line 700 – *Total Sales/Broker's Commission*. This section covers the real estate commissions paid to your and the seller's real estate agents. If neither of you were working with an agent, this would be blank. If you both were working with an agent, the commissions would be shown here. Typically, the seller pays the total real estate commission which is then split between each agent's brokerage so you would see these amounts paid from the "seller's funds" in line 703. If you were working with a buyer's agent and the seller wasn't paying the commission, you would see the amount of commission you are paying coming from the "borrower's funds" on line 703.

- Line 800 – *Items Payable in connection with Loan*. These are all of the extra fees you pay the lender, in addition to the interest they make on the loan. This is also where your mortgage broker gets paid.

- Line 1100 – *Title Charges*. The closing agent also needs to get paid, and all of the other expenses associated with the closing are covered here. There is also the fee for title insurance. I'll talk about title insurance right after POC.

Wendy's Wisdom

These things are part of most closings involving a mortgage. Whether you are buying conventionally or buying as a rent-to-own, you'll likely see these charges.

Warranty Deed

The Warranty Deed is the piece of paper that officially transfers ownership from the seller to you. This is the most important document for the seller to sign because once they do, the home is officially yours.

A Note About POC

You may see several areas marked with the letters POC; this means *Paid Outside of Closing.* You'll want to make sure you see the Option Fee and any additional Option Credits indicated on the HUD. They may be marked POC because you paid them or the seller credited them to you outside of closing.

Title Insurance

Whenever you buy a home, you purchase title insurance. Both the buyer and the seller pay for title insurance costs. Title insurance is an insurance policy that protects the title/deed of your new home. The title insurance is both necessary and a protection for you. Should there arise any problems with the title, this insurance policy is your protection. For instance, two years after closing the seller's old mortgage still shows up as a lien on your home (even though you are now the owner). The title insurance company will remove that for you. You don't have to worry about it.

Title insurance usually includes some exclusions or things that are not covered under the policy. Schedule A of the policy includes standard exclusions, and Schedule B includes non-standard exclusions.

The non-standard Schedule B exclusions will be specific to the rent-to-own home you are buying. You will want to review these more carefully.

You can, and should, request a copy of the title commitment prior to closing. The title commitment is used before closing so that anything that needs to be removed or cleaned up before the closing can be, in order to issue the final title policy to you. This is similar to the pre-title work you obtained when you screened the seller before renting the home. If you have any questions, don't hesitate to ask your closing agent.

Each state differs as to who writes the title insurance policy and who executes the closing. Some states are "attorney closing" states and others are "title company" states. In either case, the title insurance is reviewed and signed off by an attorney.

The Closing

This is where you officially purchase your rent-to-own home. You've obtained a mortgage and the seller is transferring the deed/title of the home to you.

Closings can be confusing for the average buyer or seller because they are asked to sign a lot of paperwork, but don't always understand what they are signing. You can always ask questions about anything you don't understand. Prior to the closing, if you haven't signed up for Pre-Paid Legal, you will want to do so. Your Pre-Paid Legal attorney can review all of your closing documents with you. There is usually no charge for this service. You can sign up at www.GotLegalPlans.com.

When you go to the closing, there is a mountain of paperwork. Unfortunately, most of it is for you. It's part of getting your mortgage. I think lenders don't really feel secure in giving you a loan until they have your signature on about 20,000 pieces of paper. Yes, I'm exaggerating. I think the actual number of times you have to sign is 19,999. The seller won't be signing nearly as much. For the most part, they just sign the title of the home over to you and then twiddle their thumbs while you sign everything else until they can collect their closing check.

That's it! Now that you have completed the purchase of your rent-to-own home, you have fulfilled the dream of homeownership. You've repaired your credit and you are building for your future by owning a home. Congratulations!!

PART 6:

FOR THE REAL ESTATE AGENT ONLY

Chapter 20

How to Find and Qualify Buyers

Congratulations! You are taking the time to invest in yourself and to learn how you can offer creative options to your clients and customers. You are not going to let the current market get you down - you are figuring out how to make it work for you. You are interested not only in how to *survive,* but to go above and beyond and *thrive* in a softer market. There is just as much money to be made in today's soft market as there was in a thriving market, but it is needs to be done differently. As agents, we must help our sellers who cannot sell their homes *(Rent-to-Sell)* and our buyers who cannot buy right now *(Rent-to-Buy).*

We all long for the time when we got the listing, put a sign in the ground and later that day we had three offers! Those days are gone, but I must congratulate you on being one of the few agents to dig in, get creative and get busy when necessary. It will surely pay off for you!

In down real estate markets, it becomes particularly difficult for agents to make a living if they rely entirely on conventional sales. By conventional sales, I mean the buyer that can purchase a home because they are approved for a mortgage. When this happens, it's easy to close a real estate transaction.

Down markets have a high attrition rate for real estate agents because, like so many people, they become complacent and expect business to come knocking on their door. Now, we must go door knocking, well, not literally. You can actually turn this type of market into a high transaction market for you by finding buyers and sellers where other agents don't even think to look! Believe me, they are waiting for you!

You have these prospective buyers who are coming in or calling your office, but once they are told to get "pre-approved", you don't hear back from them. Why? They go away hopeless thinking they can't buy a home. This may be true for some types of buyers, but for many, they can be turned into a buyer with some creative ideas – like Rent-to-Own/Lease Option.

What we are looking for in our buyers are good people. They are good people, but something happened to them financially and they need some time to start over. They may have lost their job, had a medical problem with no medical insurance, gone through a divorce, etc. Do not send them away! Most likely you will be able to help them after you read this book.

Wendy's Wisdom

There are many excuses we could use in today's market to explain why we are not producing like we want to. You can make money or you can make excuses, but you can't make both.

How to Find Buyers

Let's say you don't have any buyers that you are working with now and you want to find a few. I am going to show you some easy ways to find more buyers. There are three primary ways:

1. Your own listings
2. Other agent's listings
3. Finding buyers from other agents

Your Own Listings:

If you have a listing where you know the seller will consider a lease option, then you need to advertise it to find a buyer. You can use the example ads below to find a buyer. I won't go into the details in this book on how to talk to your seller; that's in my *'Rent-to-Sell'* book, but we will cover the details of finding other agents' sellers in this book.

When you run your ad to lease option your seller's home, you might end up with more buyers than homes. Well, wouldn't that be a nice problem to have? It is actually a very likely situation. What will you do with them? We need to find these buyers another home so you can get paid another commission.

Other Agent's Listings:

You can review the next chapter to find available sellers from other agents' listings. However, once you know what home you are advertising, you will do it the same way you advertise your own listings, but you won't put down the exact address or pictures of the home. You should not advertise their exact home or listing. If it is not your listing, you need to script a generic ad for the home and location. Let's go through some examples so you will see what I mean.

The following ads are ones I run in Craigslist with great response. Notice there are no addresses on the listings.

$1,295 / 3 br – Rent-to-Own Home in Brighton (Brighton)

3 bdrm / 2 bath home on over 1 acre in Brighton area… feeling of being up north-

Lease Option/Rent-to-Own – credit problems ok – must have $4,000 down for a lease option.

Call me, I have many listings for lease option in other areas –

123-456-7890 ask for Wendy

Wendy Patton with Keller Williams (NO FEE to you for my services)

$1,095 / 3 br – Lease Option or Rent-to-Own (Sterling Heights)

GREAT SUB and great school system – HURRY, this won't last. Your chance to buy a home even with poor credit.

I will help you get your credit repaired so you can again own a home – or be a first time home buyer. 3 bdrm/ 2 bath / 2 car garage and a basement

I have many homes and in many areas on lease option or land contract - $4,000 down minimum for a lease option and $7,500 minimum for a land contract

NO FEE to you for my services – Wendy with Keller Williams –

call NOW 123-456-7890 ask for Wendy

$1,295 / 3 bdrm – Rent-to-Own in Southfield - Home (Southfield)

Great home in Southfield in a VERY nice sub. It is a 3 bdrm with 2 baths and a 2 car garage. Full basement. If you can't qualify for a mortgage now and you're ready to own, then this program is for you.

Own a home and get the tax benefits of home ownership. Less than perfect credit is no problem. I can help you. $4,000 option fee up front required. I can help you get into a home NOW with no charge for this service. If you would like another area, let me know and I can find you something that will work for you.

Email me at <u>Wendy@WendyPatton.com</u> or call Keller Williams Realty.

123-456-7890 ask for Wendy

Finding Buyers From Other Agents:

I use the following letter to attract buyers from other real estate agents. Many real estate agents have people call them or come into their office that are not qualified to purchase a home. They were not able to get a "pre-approval" letter. Ever have this happen to you? What did you do? Did you show them homes for sale when you knew they were not qualified? No, of course not. Most real estate agents will not show them around either and will consider their information "garbage". I realized that other agents have these types of buyers that would work well for a lease option, but they don't know it. I put together a letter to explain how this works so agents can refer these types of buyers to me.

Of course, you can change the amount to anything you like. Also, you might not need to pay anyone anything for their buyers if you can find them free on the Internet. Use a higher payment amount to Realtors® when your market is hotter and possibly smaller amounts when your market is softer. Test it out if you need buyers.

Garbage or $500???

Dear Agent Name,   Date

Have you ever had a potential buyer come into your office and not be qualified to get a mortgage? Don't throw away their information. Refer them to us, and if we end up renting to them, we will send you $500!

So, is it a piece of garbage, or $500?

Please call us at (phone number) to get more information, but don't throw away your potential buyers that we might be able to work with. This offer is valid until (date).

Sincerely,

Your name

Fax this paper to us at: (your fax number) _____

_____   _____
Your Name (Referring Realtor®)   Your Phone number(s)

_____   _____
Your Employing Broker's Name   Name of Person
                                            Referring Broker's Name

_____   _____
Name of Person Referring   Name of Person Referring Phone
                                            number(s)

Please explain what they are looking for and where. We want to help as many people as possible: _____

Qualify Your Buyers

After you have done what you need to find a buyer, now you must screen them. You need to know if they are qualified to be a lease option buyer. You will not want to waste their time or, most importantly, yours. When I talk to a buyer on the phone, here are some of the things I will ask or discuss with them.

<u>Script to Qualify Buyers</u>

"Thanks for calling, how did you hear about us?"

(Find out where your leads are coming from)

"Great. Where are you living at now?"

"And how long have you lived there?"

"You called on the lease option property, right?"

"Okay, great. What rental price range are you looking for?"

Let them answer and then mentally multiply their answer by 3 to 4 times. For example, if they say $1,000, then their income level should be $3,000 to $4,000 so I ask,

"Okay, great. So with that rental range, I assume you make between $3,000 to $4,000 minimum, is that right?"

This is a nice way to say, "How much do you make?" without saying it that directly. If they don't earn this much, you will want to share with them that this home will probably be out of their price range, but you might be able to help them find another home.

"Why do you want to move from your current location?"

"You called about this rent-to-own/lease option home so I assume that means you have some credit issues you might need to address, is that correct? Maybe a bankruptcy or a foreclosure?"

Let them answer, and if they had a bankruptcy or foreclosure, ask when this occurred. This is important because it will determine when they can qualify for a mortgage.

If they have been through a foreclosure, find out why. If they went through a bankruptcy, ask them the circumstances. What has changed in their situation to make it better now? Snoop a bit. Most often, they will share with you, but asking questions gives you many answers. Remember to let them talk if they want to talk. When people talk, two things happen:

1. They feel comfortable with you and you will probably get their business. It builds rapport when you listen.

2. You can learn a lot about a person when you listen. This will help you determine if you can or if you want to help them with a lease option.

"How about your upfront payment – money to 'move in' – what range are you considering?"

You will want to make sure they have a good portion down. You will want to make sure they have 1-3% minimum of the purchase price. If the home is $100,000, then they need to have $1,000-3,000. If they say they only have $500, then you might want to see if they can get additional money by borrowing from a friend or family member.

"Okay. What's your time frame for finding a new place?"

If they seem qualified:

"Great. What type of property are you looking for?" (How many bedrooms, bathrooms - what are their needs and wants?)

"Okay...let me tell you about some of our properties that fit what you're looking for...and then we can schedule an appointment to see them."

If the buyers are qualified, it's time to begin the process and view the listings.

In the next chapter, I will cover how to find sellers for your rent-to-own buyers.

I always say –

"Will you be here in five years - or gone in five months?"

Only creative agents will prosper during down markets.

Chapter 21

How to Find Rent-to-Own Sellers for Your Buyers

The following "tips and tricks" are key to finding qualified sellers for your rent-to-own buyers.

Find Rent-to-Own Sellers

Do you know of any sellers who are frustrated because their house is sitting unsold? Perhaps they had to move out to live with family or they are paying two mortgages. They are tired of maintaining their empty house. They don't want to lower the price any more than they already have. If they are not upside down (owe more than it is worth), then you CAN help them put together a transaction.

Finding a seller who can do a rent-to-own for your rent-to-own buyer is critical. It's also critical for you to know how to put together this type of transaction. Any agent and any buyer can find the seller with a home listed as a "rent-to-own". Those are easy.

What this chapter focuses on is how to find sellers who are not so obvious.

Everything in this book is about working with buyers. For working with sellers, you'll want to reference my book *'Rent-to-Sell'*. Both are excellent resources and should be a part of any real estate agent's reference materials.

Here are some ways to find rent-to-own sellers:

- Newspapers and the Internet
- The MLS
    - Current Listings
    - Expired Listings
- Builders with extra inventory
- Other agents you know – networking

Let's discuss how we can use these to find sellers for rent-to-own transactions.

Newspapers and the Internet are great places to find sellers of rent-to-own properties, but not the way you might think. If you were to look in the newspaper right now, you probably will not find a long list of properties for sale with "Rent-to-Own" or "Lease Option" in the ads. You will not, if you were to look, find many on Craigslist either. You might then think the next best area to look in is the FSBO or For Sale By Owner section. You can try these sellers as well, but if you want the highest level of success from your efforts, you will want to call the "For Rent" section of the paper. What you are looking for are "motivated sellers" who had their home listed with a real estate agent, but it didn't sell so they decided to rent it. You are not looking for the landlord that intends to keep their property as an investment forever.

The MLS will give you current and expired listings, but very few of them will say, "Rent-to-Own". There are several ways to find sellers open to rent-to-own using current listings. Obviously, if you enter "Lease Option" or "Rent-to-Own" in the search criteria, you will find a few. This will produce a short list of potentials the easy way. As you can tell, I like to find the "not so obvious" listings. I don't have any competition for my buyers when no one else knows that a seller will do a rent-to-own but me. Here is the criterion that I look for to qualify listings on the MLS that are potential rent-to-owns:

- Listed over 90 days

- In the buyer's price range and area

- Homes that are not bank owned (REOs)

- Homes that are not upside down in equity or a short sale situation

- The sellers are not behind on their mortgage payments

- Homes that are vacant

Here is a script I use when calling other real estate agents about their listings:

Script for a Realtor® to Use When Calling Other Real Estate Agents

"Hi Sally (or whatever their name is – it works best if you use their real name instead of calling them all Sally*). "My name is* _____ *with* _____ (Realty Company) *and I was calling about the home you have listed at* _____ (the address). *Is it still available?"*

After they say, *"Yes"*:

"I noticed it has been listed awhile..."

I then SHUT UP. See what they say. They might say, *"Yes..."* then I would go on to the next question. Or they might start to talk more – which is what I am hoping they will do. Maybe they will tell me why it has been listed a long time or what the status is. You would be amazed at what others will tell you when you zip it and listen. The next question is,

> *"Well, I wondered if they would be open to something creative?"*

Again, I leave it at that and say nothing more. Sometimes they will run away with a long explanation of what they will or will not do or sometimes they say, *"Like what?"*

> *"Well, something like a rent-to-own or a lease option with our commissions paid in full. I have a rent-to-own buyer I'm working with. Would your seller be open to something like this?"*

Don't say anything until they respond. You'll get one of four responses.

1. *"Yes, they have mentioned that to me."*

If you get a positive response, the next question to ask is:

> *"Great, do you know what kind of terms they are looking for or are they looking for an offer?"*

If they are looking for terms that work for your buyer or they are looking for an offer, make an appointment for your buyer to look at the home. If the terms are not within your buyer's scope, then ask the following:

> *"Do you have any other listings where your seller might have said to you, 'Sally, if you don't sell my home soon, I might have to rent it,' Sally* (remember use their real name☺)*, can you think of any of your listings that might work for my buyers?"*

Sally may also respond to the rent-to-own question like this:

2. *"No, they need to sell now and wouldn't be interested in that."*

If this is the case, jump right to the question where you ask if she has any other listings that might work.

3. *"I'm not sure; I would have to check with them."*

With this response, encourage the agent to talk with her clients. Remind her that your buyer is looking for a rent-to-own home in this area and her commission would be paid in full.

Or they may respond:

4. *"What are you talking about?"*

Not all agents are familiar with the specifics of a rent-to-own. You may have to give her a brief explanation. Tell her about rent-to-own and how great it has been for increasing your business in the current real estate market.

Builders With Extra Inventory - Many builders have homes that they have built, but have not yet sold. They are sitting on inventory and it might be financially killing them. Many builders are open to a rent-to-own now. The only reason a builder might not be able to do a rent-to-own is if he has a construction loan that can't be extended or has a balloon. You will want to make sure that the builder is not in a position that will cause a problem for the sale down the road. Make sure they have spoken with their lender about a rent-to-own. You can use a similar script with the builder as you did with other real estate agents above.

Other Agents You Know – Networking is always a good way to find out about sellers who would be willing to consider renting-to-own their homes. So often, agents will talk about their frustrations with listings that "just won't sell". You hear it all the time. The agent spends Sunday afternoons holding an open house, freshly baked cookies and all. The price is as low as the sellers will tolerate. They are at a loss as to what to do. You can help! You are now armed with information that real estate agents need. These agents have made a good living and earned a great reputation through the years. However, changing times have passed them by and you can help them see things differently. Talk with them about offering their sellers the option of renting-to-own.

Which Sellers Can Usually Consider Rent-to-Own?

If you are looking through your own listings or the listings of other agents for potential candidates, think about what factors make a good rent-to-own seller. Take these factors into account as you talk to your fellow agents about their listings; you are looking for a good fit for your buyers.

Rent-to-own doesn't work for every seller. It isn't the perfect solution to every situation. That being said, there are definitely many sellers who could benefit from renting-to-own. These are the ones you want to find for your buyers, as well as to creatively get your own listings sold. Let's look at some of the criterion that makes a seller a potential fit for rent-to-own.

- *Seller has already moved into a new home.* Whether the seller bought or built a new home and the old one hasn't sold yet, they have two homes and two house payments. No seller wants to pay for a home that is sitting empty.

- *Relocated to a new area.* If a seller has relocated and the old home hasn't sold yet, as above, this is a motivated seller. Again, two house payments are too many for anyone.

- *New marriage or relationship.* If the couple were both homeowners prior to getting together, they may have a house to sell that may be a perfect rent-to-own possibility.

- *Owe as much on their home as it's worth.* This lack of

equity makes it difficult for a seller to sell as a rent-to-own, but it is possible. A rent-to-own home may bring a price premium that can cover some or all of this difference. Plus, the additional time of the rental period will allow the seller to *pay down more principal* on his mortgage. Make sure that the seller will be able to pay the entire commission at the closing.

- *Own free and clear.* Free and clear sellers aren't burdened with the extra mortgage payment, but they are also not in the position of having a home that must be sold immediately. Even if they need money from their home, they can always take out an equity loan before the rental term starts.

- *Landlord selling a rental property.* Landlords can make great rent-to-own sellers since they are already accustomed to the idea of tenants. Since the home isn't their primary residence, they aren't likely to need the money from the sale right away.

- *Inherited the property.* Recently inherited property is usually sitting empty and the heirs may not need the money right away. Many homes that are inherited have no mortgage or debt on them. Rent-to-own works well with one or two heirs involved, but when you have many heirs, it can be tricky to get them to agree on anything.

- *Vacation home or second home.* Because this isn't the seller's principal residence, the home may be sitting empty and they may be making two mortgage payments. Renting it will give the sellers some cash each month that they don't have now.

You will notice that many good rent-to-own candidates have two things in common:

1. They have a home sitting empty, and

2. They don't need the money from the sale right away. Bear in mind that there is a difference between *needing* the money (from their equity) and *wanting* it right away.

Homeowners who are selling their principal residence and still living in it are potential candidates as well, but they need to make sure that they will still be able to get a mortgage on their new home while renting their old home. Lending requirements are tougher on this type of situation than in past years. If you have a home seller in this situation, have them get pre-approved with a lender prior to listing their home as a rent-to-own. If you are representing the buyers, you should have the seller's agent do this.

Which Sellers Are Able to do Rent-to-Own, but Should Not?

We have established criteria for sellers who can consider rent-to-own, but not all of them are actually able to do it. Here are some examples of sellers who could, or would, consider rent-to-own, but who are probably not good candidates to do so. This is where protecting yourself, your buyer and the brokerage come into play. This book teaches how to work with *buyers,* and I assume you are a buyer's agent while reading this book; however, you still want to make sure it is a viable deal for all involved, and that includes the seller. If the seller thinks he can do a rent-to-own sale, but isn't actually able to, it puts your buyers in a bad situation and you need to protect them.

- *Short sale situation.* Sellers who are on the brink of foreclosure and owe more than the house is worth are not likely to be able to do rent-to-own. They might want to do this or think they can, but think about what could happen down the road when your tenant-buyer decides to buy and the seller doesn't have the money for the shortage to bring to the closing. What then? It would be a mess for sure, and we don't like messes! If they have the shortage to pay on the mortgage, then require that prior to putting a buyer into the property on a rent-to-own.

- *Behind on payments.* Sellers who are behind on payments might be okay, if they can get caught up, and are not too upside-down on their home. Sometimes, with the help of the option fee, or some other means, the seller can get caught up. In this situation, you would definitely want your buyer to make the mortgage payments directly to the mortgage company instead of trusting the seller to do so. This is crucial to make things work.

- *Live in Texas.* This is a reminder, in case you didn't catch it earlier in the book. State law in Texas makes rent-to-own home sales almost impossible for the seller. If you are working with a buyer, it can work, but do be careful that it won't end up being unfair for the seller.

Will the Rent Cover Their Mortgage?

If the seller's mortgage payments are higher than the monthly rent, he would have to cover the difference each month. Is he in a financial position to do this? It is a **must** to make this scenario work. He can do a rent-to-own if he can cover this difference. For example: if the rent is $1,200 per month and the seller's mortgage payment is $1,397 per month, the seller would need to pay $197 each month for the shortage. This is another case where it would be a good idea to set up an escrow account to ensure the mortgage is actually getting paid, to protect your buyer. The buyer would pay in $1,200 each month, and the seller would pay in $197 each month plus any escrow fee charges.

What can you do if the seller can't afford to cover the difference each month? Are your buyers out of luck with this home?

Not necessarily. Here's an idea that would involve your buyers paying more in monthly rent to cover the difference, which will work if the seller has some equity in their home. If the seller says he can't afford to cover the difference, you can ask him the following:

> *"If the buyers covered that monthly difference for you, would you be willing to give them a credit in return?"*

They will most likely answer, *"What do you mean?"*

You can explain that if the buyers pay the extra $200 ($197) per month each month in rent to cover the mortgage payment, they would want that $200 plus an additional $100 per month credited as an option credit against the purchase price of the home. This keeps the seller from having to pay out-of-pocket each month to cover the difference, but it also gives the buyer additional option credits to count towards a down payment when they buy the home.

Obviously, you should discuss this with your buyer before you bring it up to the seller. The buyer needs to understand that the option credits are forfeited if they don't buy the home. This would mean that if they chose not to buy the home, they would be paying the extra $200 per month for nothing. It may be beneficial to the buyer because it makes their rental payment closer to what a real mortgage payment would be, so they'll be accustomed to paying that amount when it comes time to buy. They also build additional equity during their rental period.

As you can see, the seller would have to have enough equity to give these option credits back to the buyer when they sell. For example, if the owner owes $200,000 on their home and your buyer is paying $220,000 for it, then they have some room to give away those credits, but if they owe $215,000 there is not enough margin to give the additional option fee credits and/or pay the commission. You will want to confirm all of this.

You, as an agent, need to be cautious of creating liability for you, the buyer, and your brokerage in everything pertaining to the rent-to-own transaction. You must protect your buyers as much as possible. However, as in any type of real estate transaction, there are always risks. Understand and explain the risks to your buyers.

In the next chapter, we will discuss the risks you need to discuss when doing a rent-to-own.

Chapter 22

Having the Rewards and Risks Discussion with Your Buyer

When you discuss rent-to-own with your buyers, you should always explain the potential risks as well as the rewards. It is important to make sure your buyers understand both so they can evaluate them as part of their decision to buy their home on a rent-to-own basis. Which one do you want first, the good or the bad news?

Okay, we will go with the bad news (the risks) before we cover the benefits. There are several risks to your buyers in a rent-to-own transaction, but with your assistance they can be minimized significantly. Actually, most of the risks reside with the buyer themselves.

How Should You Discuss Rent-to-Own With Your Buyer?

Once you find potential rent-to-own buyers, begin by giving them a brief overview of rent-to-own transactions. Even if they think they fully understand them, you'll need to discuss it with them to make sure you both are on the same page. You will also want to find out what they can afford, how much they can pay for an option fee, and so forth. Discuss the potential risks and rewards with them. Of course you'll also want to determine the basics; bedrooms, bath, area, etc.

Make sure that they understand that they are committing to a lease period, even if they choose not to buy the home. You will want to explain to them the importance of working to improve their credit during the rental period so that they can buy the home.

Talk with them about how much home they can afford. Even if they have been turned down on their loan application, they may have an idea from the loan officer of the price range they can afford. Ask them how much they are looking to pay in monthly rental payments. Make sure they understand what an Option Fee is, and ask the amount they have available. You can also present alternatives to rent-to-own to your buyers as well, such as:

- Land Contract / Contract for Deed

- Getting the seller to hold a second mortgage (if the buyer can get approved for a primary mortgage, but cannot qualify for the entire loan amount)

These techniques are something you should study and research if you want to offer your clients a full spectrum of creative ways to buy a home.

Risks & Responsibilities

Included below is a checklist that covers the potential risks and responsibilities. Don't just hand your buyers the list to initial and sign. Review and discuss each item with them. Don't over promise rent-to-own to your buyers - keep it realistic. Portray the risks in a fair light. Make sure you keep the risks based in reality, though, because they can also be pretty gloomy if a buyer misunderstands and thinks the risks are certainties.

Rent-to-own for a buyer usually goes well if they do what they are supposed to do. The risks come mostly from lack of them doing their part. If they pay rent on time, pay off their other debts, etc., it can be a great way to purchase a home. There are a few risks that can be caused by the seller. Each side must abide by all the terms and conditions in order to make the deal work smoothly. This is the same with any other type of real estate transaction. However, it is critical with a rent-to-own, since the time of the transaction is longer and more things can happen to both parties during the extended time period. The goal in this chapter is to minimize the risks for both parties.

Real estate agents, as well as their clients, can benefit tremendously from Pre-Paid Legal services. Check it out at www.GotLegalPlans.com to save legal fees and time.

Many of the risks caused by the sellers can be greatly alleviated by you if you do your due diligence in advance, such as making sure they are current on their mortgage and not "upside down", pulling pre-title work, and so on. The chances of these risks happening are fairly slim with proper planning, but they can still happen.

In an effort to protect yourself as well as the buyer, I ask buyers to sign a form including the following as part of all rent-to-own transactions through my real estate firm.

Wendy's Wisdom

This is very important. Have your broker and/or the attorney for your office review and approve this checklist before you use it with any of your clients or customers. In most states, real estate agents must review contract additions and changes with an attorney.

C.Y.A. (Cover Your ASSets)

After you discuss the rent-to-own process with your buyers and they agree that they want to go forward with a rent-to-own purchase, go one step further to cover yourself from any possible repercussions in the future.

Acknowledgments for Buyers for a Rent-to-Own Transaction

_____ I/We understand that if I do not pay my rent on time or close on the home, I will lose my option fee that I put down.

_____ I/We understand that the seller could have additional liens placed on their property during the option period which could result in the seller's inability, or delay, to sell me their home (in which case my deposit should be refundable by the seller).

_____ I/We understand that I am responsible to make sure the seller's mortgage payments are made. I have a mortgage authorization in my possession so that I can use it to check on the seller's mortgage status at any time. If the payments are not made for any reason or are late, I should make my payments directly to the lender to prevent the home from being foreclosed, which would put my option fee at risk.   (Use this IF your buyer is making their payment to the seller versus paying the lender directly.)

_____ I/We understand that getting a mortgage approval prior to my option period ending is my responsibility and my risk. The option fee is non-refundable.

_____ I/We understand that the seller and real estate agents involved have nothing to do with the mortgage industry or my ability to receive a mortgage on this home. I agree to hold them harmless.

_____ I/We understand that the seller might refuse to sell the home at the time I am ready to buy. The remedies for this are in the Sales Contract, but I should contact an attorney if this happens.

_____ I/We understand that the seller does not have to extend or offer any type of seller financing or perks at the time of closing. All agreements signed at the beginning of the rental term will stand.

_____ I/We understand that I must carry a renter's insurance policy to protect my personal property in the home.

_____ I/We have sought the advice of a mortgage broker and attorney prior to signing contracts with the seller and this addendum.

_____ I/We have read everything above and understand and accept all risks and responsibilities.

_____ I/We will hold the broker (XYZ) harmless from all errors and omissions in this rent-to-own transaction.

_____*Dated* _____ *Dated*

Buyer Signature   Co-Buyer Signature

You can download the above list at www.WendyPatton.com/checklist

Review of These Risks and Responsibilities

Let's go over each statement in the Acknowledgement to clarify them.

> *I/We understand that if I do not pay my rent on time or close on the home I will lose my option fee that I put down.*

The Option Agreement is contingent upon the tenant-buyer fulfilling his obligations. These include paying rent, paying it on time and purchasing the home. While the tenant-buyer is not obligated to purchase the home, he will forfeit his option fee if he doesn't. He will also forfeit his option fee if he violates the terms of the lease, such as not paying the rent on time.

It is very easy for a tenant-buyer to protect their option fee. All they really need to do is be good tenants and then buy the home. It's completely within their control.

> *I/We understand that the seller could have additional liens placed on their property during the option period which could result in the seller's inability, or delay, to sell me their home (in which case my deposit should be refundable by the seller).*

This is a no-no for sellers. They shouldn't be jeopardizing their ability to sell their home during the option period. However, just because they aren't supposed to do it doesn't mean it never happens. Certainly, most rent-to-own sellers won't get in this position. Also, your tenant-buyer can help protect themselves by recording the Memorandum of Option. This will prevent the seller from being able to have certain liens placed against the home, such as refinancing, during the rental period.

While instances of a seller having their title clouded during the option period are rare, they can happen. It is something that the tenant-buyer should be aware of as a potential risk.

> *I/We understand that I am responsible to make sure the seller's mortgage payments are made. I have a mortgage authorization in my possession so that I can use it to check on the seller's mortgage status at any time. If the payments are not made for any reason or are late, I should make my payments directly to the lender to prevent the home from being foreclosed, which would put my option fee at risk. (Use this IF your buyer is making their payment to the seller versus paying the lender directly.)*

Getting a mortgage authorization signed from the seller can

be a HUGE measure of protection for your tenant-buyer. Whenever possible, I also recommend that the tenant-buyer make their payments directly to the seller's lender from the onset – that is, I recommend this if you are the buyer's agent. At the very minimum, the buyer should insist on proof of payment from the seller every month.

If the tenant-buyer isn't making the payment directly to the lender from the beginning, they should do so at the first sign of payment troubles as they check on the status of the seller's loan. Make sure it is written into the contract that the tenant-buyer has the right to do this.

This is a big CYA for you and your brokerage, as well as protecting your buyer. Most sellers, obviously, don't intend to pocket the money and let their home go into foreclosure, however, sometimes circumstances change for sellers. For example, what if the seller lost their job? They might start keeping the rent money and not paying their mortgage. This is why it's best for the tenant-buyer to pay the lender directly from the onset. But as I said, if they can't do that, they should definitely have the ability to verify that the mortgage payments are being made.

I/We understand that getting a mortgage approval prior to my option period ending is my responsibility and my risk. The option fee is non-refundable.

If the tenant-buyer needs to improve their credit to qualify for a mortgage, you want to make sure they take the appropriate steps. Get them to sign up for credit repair. While they are not obligated to purchase the home, you definitely don't want them to lose the ability to purchase simply because they never got around to improving their credit.

You also want to stay in touch with your buyers during the

rental period to make sure they are on track. Have them check in periodically with their loan officer as well. It doesn't take much effort to check in with your buyers to make sure things are moving along. An added benefit is that they'll appreciate it, and that is the type of service that is likely to get you referrals.

> *I/We understand that the seller and real estate agents involved have nothing to do with the mortgage industry or my ability to receive a mortgage on this home. I agree to hold them harmless.*

Mortgage rules change constantly, and the current credit crunch is making it much more difficult to qualify. While you want to do what you can to help your buyer, it's important that they understand that neither you nor the seller have any control over their ability to obtain a mortgage.

> *I/We understand that the seller might refuse to sell the home at the time I am ready to buy. The remedies for this are in the Sales Contract, but I should contact an attorney if this happens.*

Just as you don't have any control over your buyer's ability to get a mortgage, you also don't have any control if the seller balks at selling the home. This is definitely something the buyer should discuss with an attorney. You can recommend Pre-Paid Legal to them if they don't already have it.

Obviously, the seller is supposed to honor their end of the bargain. They signed legal contracts saying they will do just that. One instance where a seller might try to back out of the deal is if the home has appreciated significantly. At this point, the seller may see the opportunity to sell it for more money. This is where it is important to have strong contracts that protect your buyers so they have options and can pursue them with the help of an attorney. Their recourse, if this happens, is a suit against the seller for specific performance.

> *I/We understand that the seller does not have to extend or offer any type of seller financing or perks at the time of closing. All agreements signed at the beginning of the rental term will stand.*

Most often this would come up if the buyer discovers they have to pay more in closing costs than they anticipated. They might ask for seller assistance. The seller is not obligated to grant any assistance if it wasn't in writing with the original contracts. In most cases, it would be to the seller's advantage to do this so they can get their home sold, but it isn't mandatory.

You should have your tenant-buyer check with their mortgage broker BEFORE signing contracts to determine if they will need closing cost assistance or any other seller assistance. If they do, the buyer should ask for it as part of their negotiations. You might also want to speak to their lender so that you can put any seller concessions in the contract from day one. This would ensure that they are covered the best way possible at the beginning, instead of waiting until they are trying to close on the home.

> *I/We understand that I must carry a renter's insurance policy to protect my personal property in the home.*

It is important for your buyer to understand that the seller's homeowner's insurance policy does not cover the buyer's possessions in any way. The seller's policy only covers the dwelling. Your tenant-buyer should obtain renter's insurance to protect his belongings.

I/We have sought the advice of a mortgage broker and attorney prior to signing contracts with the seller and this addendum.

If the tenant-buyer has any legal questions, they should have them answered by an attorney. We, as real estate agents, cannot provide legal advice.

You definitely want to make sure they've talked with a mortgage broker. This is a critical component to taking the necessary steps towards getting a mortgage at the end of the lease period. You want to make sure they have taken this step. Otherwise, there really isn't much point of doing a rent-to-own, they should just be tenants.

I/We have read everything above and understand and accept all risks and responsibilities.

This basically pulls it all together and states that they understand what they are getting into and accept that it may not turn out trouble free. We certainly try to do all we can to minimize the risks, but it's impossible to guarantee a perfect transaction.

I/We will hold the broker (XYZ) harmless from all errors and omissions in this rent-to-own transaction.

Put your broker name in place of the XYZ. It will be better protection for you and your company ☺. This is just one of our great "C.Y.A." clauses we need as real estate agents and brokers.

Benefits to the Home Buyer

It is important to cover the benefits to the tenant-buyer as well. You might want to start out with these, or you might want to end with these. It will depend on your approach and your buyer's style. Help them to understand how rent-to-own can get them into a home now, when it might not otherwise be possible for them to purchase a home at this time. I cover many benefits throughout this book, but here I'm going to focus on four primary ones.

1. Get into a home now

This is a fantastic benefit! How else can they live in the home they want to buy before they can qualify for financing? This gives them options! Most people who want to buy a home, but get turned down for a mortgage think they have no options. Rent-to-own is a great option for these would-be buyers.

If you can explain this option to would-be buyers who think they can't get a home, you will jump far above your competition. Very likely, your competing agent doesn't think there is anything he can do to help these buyers – and there are a lot of them out there who don't – but you can.

2. Improve their credit while they are living in the new home of their choice

This is far better than having to simply rent while repairing their credit in order to qualify for a mortgage. They are already in the home. This way they can stay focused on their goal because they see it every day.

If they can negotiate option credits, they will actually be building up a down payment through their rental payments! Not only that, but the option credits are usually significantly higher than the principal pay down would be on a mortgage, so they can build equity faster than if they bought outright.

3. The ability to lock in a price now

At the time I am writing this, home prices have been dropping in many areas, but the declines will soon be slowing and after they level out, they'll rise again. There is no better time to lock in a price than when prices are down. Even if prices are rising, it's best to lock in the price now, so that when the value goes up, their price will remain unchanged.

Without rent-to-own, your buyer wouldn't be able to take advantage of current home prices. They would have to wait until they could qualify to buy, and by then, they'll have missed a great opportunity.

4. The ability to build up equity before the closing

In the contracts, it is important to negotiate that a buyer receives some "Option Credits" each month from their rental payment. This was discussed in more detail in the earlier parts of the book, but this is one of the key benefits to a buyer. If the rent payment is $1,000 per month and the buyer gets $1,000 per month for credit, this is HUGE for the buyer. Let's say the seller won't give $1,000 per month, but will give $300 per month. This is still great as it gives your buyer $3,600 extra towards the purchase price and their down payment for one year of the option (12 months X $300 per month = $3,600). This works only when the seller has some equity in the home (these are the only sellers I recommend working with anyway).

So, you now have buyers who are interested in rent-to-own or you've had someone approach you who can't qualify for a mortgage and would be a good candidate for rent-to-own. You now know how you can help them, but are you worried about how and when you will be paid? I am sure you are. After all, as much as we like to help our buyers, we still want to get paid for our work. We will discuss how you get paid in the next chapter.

Chapter 23

How to Get Paid Your Entire Commission

and More

Don't tell me you flipped to this chapter before Chapter 1? I'll bet some of you did. While getting paid is crucial for everyone, you might want to find out more about what all this means and how it's transacted before you worry about how to get paid.  Getting paid is crucial for everyone. I can help you figure out how to make 100% of your earned commission (and potentially more), where you might otherwise have lost a buyer or just received a rental commission.

The reality is that conventional sales are difficult right now. It isn't enough to just get listings and put them on the market. Most listings aren't selling. The number of licensed agents will continue to drop as the market stays down. The main reason? It's not because there are not enough real estate transactions, but because too many agents are not willing to learn what must be done in today's market. They do not *shift* with the market. By the way, I recommend a great book by Gary Keller, Jay Papasan and Dave Jenks – _"SHIFT: How Top Real Estate Agents Tackle Tough Times"_. Make sure you add this book to your reading and reference list.

Some agents are whining and making excuses versus getting out there and figuring out how to make things work. Obviously, you are not one of them if you are reading this book. Congratulations, you are learning so you can keep earning. ☺

We, as agents, have gotten lazy. I will try not to get on a soapbox, but since I am writing this book, it gives me a little leeway. Most real estate agents rarely come to their office meetings. They rarely go to training to learn new concepts. What I talk about in this book, I teach to real estate offices across the country. When I am scheduled to speak to a real estate office, they invite their agents for weeks and weeks to come to my training session. Ninety short minutes of training and only 20% of their office will show up. Why? Because most agents won't do what they need to do to be successful in this market. I have recently talked to some office owners, and they say it is not the 80/20 rule any longer on production, but a 90/10, 10% of their agents do about 90% of the business.

If you want to keep succeeding in this business, you must adapt. Not only are rent-to-owns going to be very popular, but seller financing is also making a big come back. (That is a topic for another book.) Agents who offer rent-to-own to their buyers (and sellers) will have much more success selling homes than agents that try to hold out for only conventional, qualified buyers.

Wendy's Wisdom

You'll be able to sell more homes and help more buyers when you know how to do what this book teaches. Ultimately, you will get paid more than your fellow real estate agents.

How many times have you had a prospective buyer call or walk into your office and you ask them, *"Have you spoken to a mortgage lender? Are you pre-approved?"*

They say, *"No, I haven't talked to one yet."*

A typical agent's answer would be, *"Well, why don't you talk to a lender. Do you have one or do you want me to give you the name and phone number of one?"*

What usually happens here? You never hear from them again. Why? They probably talked to the lender and found out they were not qualified. Or, maybe they thought they were not qualified due to some credit issues they have so they've never even spoken with a mortgage broker. Maybe they rented a home instead of buying, and now the commission on that deal is lost, probably forever, for you. Not to mention the fact that the house they might have rented-to-own still sits in wait of a buyer, and your buyer is paying rent without hope of buying his own home in the foreseeable future. Sad.

How can you prevent losing those buyers and the commission? When the person says *"No,"* because they are not pre-approved, instead say, *"Okay, no problem. I am not trying to be nosey, but in order to help you the most I need to ask you a few things. Do you think you can qualify for a mortgage now or do you have any credit problems?"* If they say they don't know, or yes they do have credit issues, reassure them right away that you probably can still help them buy a home!

The goal at this point is to get a bona fide rent-to-own buyer. Obviously, if the person is capable of getting a conventional mortgage now, you'd just complete a regular sale with them, unless they specifically want to rent-to-own.

Remember my "Garbage or $500" letter from Chapter 20? You don't need to only do this with the potential buyers that contact you; you can also turn other agents' "worthless" leads into full buyers for you.

How to Get Paid Your Entire Commission

Losing out on potential buyers or only getting a rental commission isn't very appealing. Consider this instead:

With a rent-to-own sale, you still receive your full commission (and maybe more, which I'll get into shortly), plus your buyer – who didn't think they'd be able to get a home now – can get a home right away.

However, there is a string attached; you'll only get part of your commission up front (but still more than if you just placed them into a rental property), and the remainder when your tenant-buyer closes on the home.

Change the Listing Agreement

In some cases, you may find your buyer a home that is already listed as rent-to-own so the listing agent will most likely have the commission split defined in the MLS listing. In the case where it isn't already listed as a rent-to-own, and the sellers agree to sell their home as a rent-to-own to your buyer, you will need to have the listing agent get the listing agreement changed with the sellers to reflect payment for a rent-to-own. Any changes they make should be verified by your broker and, if necessary, your office's legal counsel. Here are some of the changes they'll need to make. Usually, they can be typed on a one page addendum, or handwritten in, and signed by the broker and the seller:

- Seller agrees to pay listing broker X% commission of the purchase price if listing broker secures a rent-to-own tenant-buyer by X:00 p.m., dd/mm/yy.

- Seller agrees to pay commission to listing office even if

tenant-buyer's rent-to-own agreement is extended one or more times.

No matter when your tenant-buyer closes, you still get paid – even if it is ten years from now.

- Seller agrees to pay listing broker X% of the contract purchase price from proceeds of the Option Fee received from the tenant-buyer at the time the tenant-buyer moves in.

Of course, this is negotiable between the listing agent and their seller, but it's what I recommend because most buyers only have 1-3% down. Any money above the amount set that is paid by your tenant-buyer would be retained by the seller. This would apply towards the entire commission due on this home, if and when, the tenant-buyer closes.

Since you are the buyer's agent in this case, you might want to suggest that you split what your buyer puts down for that last clause. Find this out first so you and the listing agent can split it towards your commission. Just make sure it is in writing. I often recommend having an attorney prepare a Promissory Note covering the balance of the commission payment(s) and have the seller sign it. If you are the buyer's agent only and it is not your listing, you will want to make sure the above happens BEFORE you show the home to your buyer and get them all excited, only to find out that you might not be entitled to any commission or will receive your commission at a later date. Just like we tell our clients in real estate, the same applies to us; everything in real estate must be in writing.

Wendy's Wisdom

I often recommend having an attorney prepare a Promissory Note covering the balance of the commission payment(s) and have the seller sign it. Just like we tell our clients in real estate, "Everything in real estate must be in writing."

How to Get MORE than Your "Normal" Commission

Okay, so there is no "normal" commission in real estate, but let's discuss the idea of getting a little more then your personal standard when you do a rent-to-own. How, you ask? One possibility is for the listing agent to work out a modification to the listing agreement where the seller agrees to pay the full commission (with a portion paid up front and the remainder at the end – per what we just discussed above) AND pay the first month's rent as a *rental commission.*

Why would the seller agree to do this? This is an upgraded level of service not offered by many other agents. It's a way for a seller to get their home sold when it was otherwise just sitting and costing them money each month. Adding on the rental commission could be considered a premium for the additional services being provided.

The seller's agent and seller may or may not agree to this. You can also suggest to the seller's agent that the commission be paid both from the option fee and the first month's rent. The amount of the commission isn't increasing, but you are both getting paid more in advance.

Now that you understand how you'll get paid, go back to Chapter 1 and read the entire book (if you skipped ahead☺) so you can help your buyers accomplish this type of transaction.

Be different and take this market on! Don't allow this market to take you. I always say, "You can make excuses, or you can make money, but you cannot do both." In this book, I have given you the  information you need to help buyers that are not currently qualified to get a mortgage. This will help you get more business and make more money. It will also help so many buyers realize the dream of home ownership, that otherwise would not have been able to do so. I am so glad you made the choice to read this book. Thanks!

If you never take a risk, you will never reap the reward.

Appendix A

Helpful Resources

Available at www.WendyPatton.com

- *'Rent-to-Sell'* Course - Contracts for sellers doing a rent-to-own, with audio CDs containing step-by-step instructions

- *'Rent-to-Buy'* Course - Contracts for buyers doing a rent-to-own, with audio CDs containing step-by-step instructions

- Realtor® and mortgage broker contacts for your area

- Credit repair contacts for you

- **FREE** downloads of the checklists from this book at

  www.WendyPatton.com/Checklists

- **FREE** articles on rent-to-own

Other Sites:

- www.cpsc.gov/cpscpub/pubs/426.pdf
  Protect your family from lead in your home pamphlet. Must be given to buyers and renters as part of Lead Based Paint Disclosure

- www.Craigslist.org
  A resource for buying your rent-to-own home. Also a good resource for finding free or inexpensive home improvement materials and moving boxes.

- www.familywatchdog.us/default.asp
  Free search for convicted sex offenders by name or location.

- www.freecycle.org
  A good resource for finding free home improvement materials and moving boxes.

- Pre-Paid Legal www.GotLegalPlans.com
  For affordable legal assistance with no contract required.

- www.RenttoOwnCreditRepair.com
  A great source for credit repair. Sign up as soon as you find your home.

Please feel free to email my office with **<u>success stories</u>** of buying your home using my Rent-to-Buy system. Email my office at: <u>success@wendypatton.com</u>.

Share with us in this format:

Subject Line: Success Story for Rent-to-Buy

1. Your name(s):

2. What city you live in:

3. What you did to buy your home:

4. Explain how Rent-to-Buy helped your buy your dream home:

5. May I use your name(s) and success story on my website to share with others who need Rent-to-Buy as a solution to buy their home?

Continue Your Education

Now that you know how to do rent-to-own as a buyer, would you like to learn how to do this as a seller?

If so, you can purchase *'Rent-to-Sell'* (for sellers) on my website at www.WendyPatton.com.

You can also do rent-to-owns as a **little-to-no-money-down real estate investing technique**. If you are interested in real estate investing, you can receive a FREE CD from me one of three ways:

- You can sign up for the FREE CD at: www.WendyPatton.com or

- You can email your contact information to: support@wendypatton.com

- You can also fax the following form to: 248-605-4044.

Wendy, please rush me my free CD!

Name: _____

Email: _____

Are you a Realtor®?   Yes   or   No

What Company:_____

Address: _____

City: _____

State: _____Zip: _____

Cell phone: _____

Daytime phone:_____

What are your goals for learning to invest in real estate?

_____

_____

_____

_____

About the Author...

Wendy Patton

Wendy Patton is widely recognized as one of the most inspiring speakers on "Little or No Money Down" real estate investing. Her real estate savvy, great depth of experience and viable knowledge has helped her in orchestrating the most complete and easy to follow Lease Option & Subject To program in the country.

After graduating from the University of Colorado, Wendy went to work for EDS. Soon after, she had an enlightening experience in real estate (lease/option) and walked away from her corporate job to focus her efforts on real estate investing full-time.

Wendy is a licensed real estate broker in 3 states and a licensed builder in Michigan. With over 24 successful years in general real estate and hundreds of transactions using lease option or renting-to-own, she is the country's leading expert on lease options and working with Realtors® to acquire lease option deals. Wendy loves to teach others and assist them to achieve the same level of success that she has personally experienced.

Wendy Patton is a published author and well known public speaker. Her first book, *"Investing in Real Estate with Lease Options and Subject To Deals"*, has received rave reviews on Amazon.com and other real estate investor websites. Her second book came out and was immediately a #1 Best Seller on Amazon.com. *"How to Make Hard Cash in a Soft Real Estate Market"*. She also recently appeared on HGTV's, *My House is Worth What?*

Wendy has been an educator and speaker on real estate investing since 1995. She is an avid golfer and currently lives in the Detroit suburb of Clarkston, Michigan, with her husband, Michael Gott, and their 5 children.

For more information on Wendy Patton, please visit

www.WendyPatton.com.

Have you read...

Rent to Sell

Your Hands-on Guide to SELL

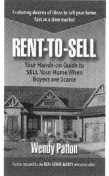

RENT-TO-SELL
Your Hands-on Guide to
SELL Your Home When
Buyers are Scarce

Wendy Patton

Essential Tools, Advice and Tips you need to give your home the edge over the competition (without spending a fortune.)

•• Step by step instructions to advertise, stage, find and qualify a buyer, and negotiate to close

•• Free downloads - checklists, articles and samples you must have

•• How to sell a fixer-upper for the highest price possible

•• Marketing secrets to get your house noticed — for free or almost free

•• How to choose and work with a real estate agent

•• Contracts and special clauses to protect you in the transaction

•• Easy ideas to get your buyer to the closing table so your home is **SOLD!**

Real Estate Agents:

This book is for you! It will teach you how to help your sellers sell their homes AND get you paid your entire commission and possibly more!

Order all of Wendy Patton's book today!
Visit
www.wendypatton.com

Made in the USA
Lexington, KY
26 April 2013